**Earn Gift Voucher for your valued opinion!**

Thank you for purchasing our Flash Cards. We are dedicated to making the 11+ & SATS experience most enriching for children & pa[...]

Your comments are important because they give us the oppo[...] improve our product. If you have found the product helpful, pl[...] moment to post a positive review on Amazon and a chance t[...]

If you feel we could have done better, then please ema[...] info@ejoycation.co.uk.

Check out our other products for 11+

CW00552413

### Mathematics Flash Cards

- ✓ A structured approach to help illustrate and master complex mathematical concepts.
- ✓ Includes challenging questions with full explanatory answers, to stimulate the young brains.
- ✓ Covers tested content for 11+ exams (CEM/GL/Independent) & SATs.

### Vocabulary Flash Cards

- ✓ 200 high-frequency words that have appeared in recent 11+ papers
- ✓ Each word meaning explained in child-friendly definition, used in a sentence, and lists synonyms / antonyms.
- ✓ Over 1300 words listed as synonyms & antonyms

Available at Amazon, leading online bookstores and directly from our website.

Visit: www.ejoycation.co.uk

# 11+ & SATS: FICTION & NON-FICTION WRITING

## First Edition

ISBN: 978-0-9931570-3-5

Visit http://bit.ly/2lwwTsJ or scan QR code to

**download free 11 plus material**

Copyright © 2019 by Ejoycation Flash Cards®

www.ejoycation.co.uk

Acknowledgements: The author and publisher are grateful to the copyright holders for permission to use quoted materials and images. All images © Shutterstock.com.

Thank you for purchasing Ejoycation Creative Writing Flash Cards.

This pack is designed to help you improve your writing and tackle 'blank page syndrome'. Topics for Fiction & Non-Fiction are given in a clear and a simple way with numerous examples and exercises to practice your learning. Structure and features are explained for Non-Fiction writing and descriptive techniques are explained with examples for Fiction writing.

Writing about just what you know is not enough. Use topics like – daily experiences, a memorable holiday, ten interesting facts about yourself, your zodiac sign and why your zodiac fits you and so on. If you need a phone, game or a computer, write a persuasive letter to your parents convincing them to do the same. Read daily as reading builds vocabulary and provides nourishment for writing.

The key is to write regularly and diligently. A little practice every day makes a big difference.

**S**pellings, **P**unctuation and **G**rammar check at the end of every piece is important. Without a SPAG check the piece is incomplete.

Use this pack to study, revise, apply and succeed.

Try these techniques to maximise your success:
- Read a card and then have a friend ask you what the term means
- Draw a picture or a diagram of what the card describes
- Create a piece of writing using the terms of a particular card
- Stick the card(s) you are revising somewhere you will see them every day, such as above your desk

If you have any questions or comments, please write to us at **info@ejoycation.co.uk**.

# Index

# Index

# Index

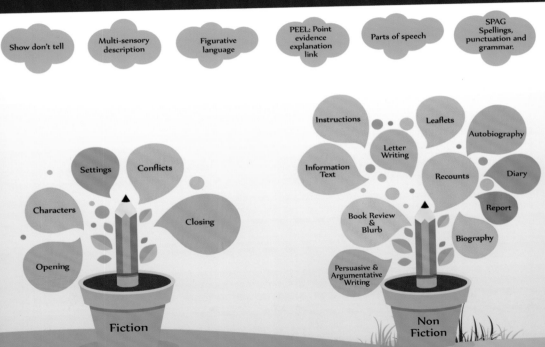

Before you start any piece of writing, plan your Purpose, Audience and Form. This will help you to identify your strategies.

**Recognise & Plan PAF**

**Purpose:** *why are you writing?*

- Argue
- Entertain
- Express
- Inform
- Instruct
- Persuade
- Recount
- Report

**Audience:** who are you writing for? How will you appeal to different groups?

- Age/Gender
- Interests
- Location
- Wealth
- Teachers
- Head Teacher
- Peers
- Family
- Community
- Parents

**Form:** what form are you writing in?

- Article
- Advertisement
- Blog
- Blurb
- Book review
- Email
- Flyer
- Leaflet
- Letters
- Report

**Fictional Writing** has a free-spirited approach. It is a more entertaining and colourful way to express the ideas, feelings, opinions or imagination of the author.

**Non-Fiction Writing** is meant to remain objective and follow a step-by-step process. It mostly follows a specific format to achieve a specific goal. The goal can be to either to motivate, inform, or influence the reader. The authors use their creativity to make it more appealing to the reader.

The two forms of writing have similarities and differences; but ultimately, one cannot exist without the other. If an author intends to motivate or educate his audience, he needs to have the creativity and imagination to attract the audience's attention.

- Fictional writing is based on imagination rather than facts.

- The writer may set a fictional story in a real setting. Example: Stories set in Stone Age.

- Fictional writing is often meant to entertain the reader rather than provide information.

- Genres (types) include adventure, comedy, drama, fantasy, horror, mystery, mythology, romance, historical fiction, science fiction (Sci-fi), tragedy.

- Non-fiction is factual writing about real events, rather than made-up stories.

- Non-fiction writing can have many different purposes such as to persuade the reader, provide information, recount of an event, writing review of a book or a movie and are written for a variety of audience.

- Types of Non-fiction writing include reports (chronological and non-chronological), persuasive writing, advertisements, diary writing, autobiography, biography, information text, reviews, letters, newspaper and magazine articles.

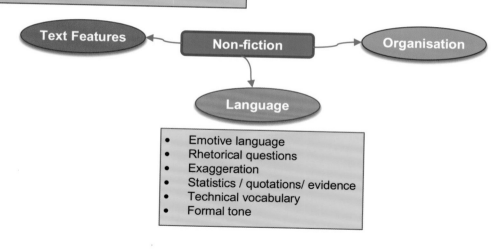

- Font: plain, bold, italics, underline
- Title: headings, subheadings
- Bullet points
- Diagrams, photographs, illustrations
- Charts, tables, graphs
- Maps
- Timelines

- Index
- Table of contents
- Glossary
- Preface
- Bibliographic reference

**Text Features** ← **Non-fiction** → **Organisation**

↓

**Language**

- Emotive language
- Rhetorical questions
- Exaggeration
- Statistics / quotations/ evidence
- Technical vocabulary
- Formal tone

Figurative language is the use of words and expressions in a non-literal sense. It makes a piece of writing more dramatic and interesting.

Figurative language can be found anywhere from poems to songs or even day-to-day conversations. There are many forms of figurative language.

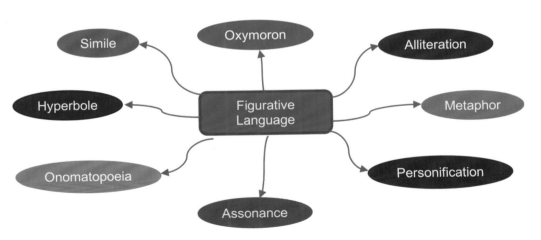

A simile is a technique used to compare something with something else using "like" or "as".

- He was <u>as</u> cunning <u>as</u> a fox.
- My heart shivered <u>like</u> sails in the wind.
- The buzz on the street was <u>like</u> the buzzing of flies.
- Their breath was rising <u>like</u> steam.
- The truth was <u>like</u> a bad taste on his tongue.
- She hung her head <u>like</u> a dying flower.
- My soul is lost and tossed <u>like</u> a ship on a shoreless sea.
- The soldiers were <u>as</u> brave <u>as</u> lions.
- The pirate was <u>as</u> crooked <u>as</u> a witch's hat.
- Her lovely hair was <u>as</u> black <u>as</u> coal.
- The news of her death made my heart <u>as</u> heavy <u>as</u> lead.

Can you think of some examples of your own?

A figure of speech that compares one thing to another directly. The only difference between metaphor and simile is that metaphor does not use "as" or "like".

- Her eyes were glistening jewels.
- She was feeling blue after her friends left.
- My kids are my sunshine.
- The mind is an ocean.
- The world is a stage.
- He was a speeding bullet.
- He drowned in a sea of grief.
- He listened to their conversation with a wooden face.
- In the absence of the teacher, the classroom was a zoo.
- During the rush hours, M25 is a parking lot.

Can you think of some examples of your own?

**The hyperbole is the technique that uses exaggeration to prove a point or to describe something.**

- My car goes faster than the speed of light.
- He was taller than the Shard.
- She was brighter than the sun.
- If I do not get the new X-Box I will die.
- I have a ton of chores to do.
- My birthday will never come.
- I could listen to my favourite song forever.
- I was almost killed of boredom in the lesson.
- No one can beat him in the game of Chess.
- I am so happy as the maths test today was the easiest test in the world.

Can you think of some examples of your own?

Personification is a technique that gives human attributes or actions to objects.

- At 7:00am, my **alarm clock springs** into life.
- My **computer throws** a fit every time I try and use it.
- The **trees crept** closer and closer.
- The **sun smiled** down on us.
- The **trees whispered** around us.
- The **stars danced** in the moonlit sky
- Lightning **danced** across the sky.
- **Time creeps** up on you.
- The **fire ran** wild.
- The **wind howled** in the night.

Can you think of some examples of your own?

# Onomatopoeia

**Onomatopoeia are words that imitate the sound they spell.**

- The foliage underneath my feet **cracked** and **crunched**.
- I **banged** on the drum as hard as I could during the music lesson.
- The **clanging** pans and pots woke up the baby.
- The bird's **chirp** filled the empty night air.
- The ferocious **buzz** of the bees made me move further into the woods.
- Her heels **clicked** as she walked on the hardwood floor.
- The dishes fell to the floor with a **clatter**.
- The hail **pattered** on the tin roof.
- The rain slowed down to a soft **pitter-patter**.
- I **ripped** open my Christmas presents.
- The thirsty cat **slurped** the milk from its bowl.
- The firemen **squirted** water on the wildfire.

Can you think of some examples of your own?

Alliteration is the repetition of the first sound(s) in two or more words that follow each other. These words may be adjacent or may be separated by a word or even a few words.

- Carrie's cat clawed her couch creating chaos.
- Silent sleeping souls surrounded me.
- The dirty dozen destroyed the den.
- Nick needed new notebooks.
- Kim's kids keep kicking.
- The Fantastic Four flew to fame.
- Sara's six sisters slept soundly.
- Mike's microphone made mad music for his mates.
- I boarded the American Airline and ate my appetizing apple.

Can you think of some examples of your own?

# Oxymoron

**Oxymoron is a figure of speech with a combination of two contradicting words.**

- The **plastic glasses** were cheaper.
- I was told to **act naturally**.
- I had to go through the **pain for pleasure**.
- The boy was **clearly confused**.
- London was in the **great depression**.
- The joke was **seriously funny**.
- I gave an **exact estimate** to the builder.
- I distinctly **remember forgetting** that.
- My friend was **found missing** after the disaster.
- We were told that the handbags were **original copies**.
- UK has one of the strongest **peace forces** in the world.

Can you think of some examples of your own?

**Assonance is the repetition of vowel sounds in nearby words. It is sometimes called an internal rhyme.**

- Let the cat out of the bag.
- "I must confess that in my quest I felt depressed and restless."
- Men sell the wedding bells.
- A stitch in time saves nine.
- Honesty is the best policy.
- The early bird catches the worm.

Can you think of some examples of your own?

**Complete the sentences and identify the figure of speech in use.**

1. The wolves _____ at the moon.
2. Her illness made her as _____ as a ghost.
3. Her dance was as _____ as a swan.
4. _____ Charlie chose a chunky chutney.
5. Bianca baked a big cake for the ___ bash.
6. The joke was _____ funny and left us all dissolved in laughter.
7. He found the direction clearly _____.
8. The good news was _____ to the ears.
9. Her brain is the size of a _____.
10. The computers at our school are _____.
11. The _____ clouds _____ across the sky.
12. It was hot and dry and the grass ___ for water.
13. My little brother loves to _____ on the drum.

Complete the sentences and identify the figure of speech in use?

1. The wolves howled at the moon. (Onomatopoeia)
2. Her illness made her as pale as a ghost. (Simile)
3. Her dance was as graceful as a swan. (Simile)
4. Cheeky Charlie chose a chunky chutney. (Alliteration)
5. Bianca baked a big cake for the birthday bash. (Alliteration)
6. The joke was seriously funny and left us all dissolved in laughter. (Oxymoron)
7. He found the directions clearly confusing. (Oxymoron)
8. The good news was music to the ears. (Metaphor)
9. Her brain is the size of a pea. (Hyperbole)
10. The computers at our school are dinosaurs. (Hyperbole)
11. The lazy clouds sailed across the sky. (Personification)
12. It was hot and dry and the grass begged for water. (Personification)
13. My little brother loves to bang on the drum. (Onomatopoeia)

**Techniques**

**Following section illustrates techniques to improve your creative writing by making it more vivid. This helps the readers to paint a picture in their minds and stay hooked on to your piece of writing.**

1. Use *specific* and *concrete* details. The reader can more easily identify with specific details. Here, the details are required to impress upon the reader, the luxury and opulence associated with the product.

*The metallic red Mercedes S3000 with its 600 HP engine sneers at the speed limits: powerful, smooth and exceptionally agile. The soft leather seats and the walnut wood trim give luxury a new definition.*

*The chronograph features along with the luxurious 18ct gold case and bracelet makes the timepiece extremely stylish and desirable. It's intricate detailing is second to none!*

**Techniques**

2. Use *sensory details* by adding all five senses. The more you can create a multisensory world for your reader, the more they will be engaged.

*On my way to the school, I tightened my duffel coat as the cool and crisp breeze refreshed everything it caressed. The red, yellow and orange leaves floated gracefully as they fell to the ground. I treaded slowly, crunching the foliage below. The aroma of the apple pie from coming the neighbour's garden piqued my hunger.*

3. Use appropriate *figures of speech* including metaphor, simile, alliteration.

4. Use a *mixture of both showing and telling* and do not overwhelm the reader with too many descriptions. Keep your piece vivid yet keep moving on to the main plot of your story.

**Telling** is passive and does not engage the reader enough.

**Showing**, however, is active and creates mental images that bring your story and characters to life.

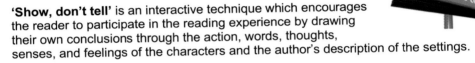

'**Show, don't tell**' is an interactive technique which encourages the reader to participate in the reading experience by drawing their own conclusions through the action, words, thoughts, senses, and feelings of the characters and the author's description of the settings.

### Examples

**Tell:** He was very angry.
**Show:** He clenched his fists shaking violently and cursing in his head.

**Tell:** She was so happy.
**Show:** She had a bounce in her step as she walked across the hall and her grin stretched from ear to ear.

**Tell:** He was very nervous.
**Show:** His voice cracked and palms got sweaty as he took the shallow breaths.

**Tell:** I was scared.
**Show:** My hearth was thumping and my mouth was as dry as Sahara Desert.

**Example 1:** I have a classmate called Kale and he is a big bully. I feel very angry and frustrated when I see him. Once I could not control my anger and retaliated back.

**Improved:** Kale saw me and smacked me on my head. It was not the first time and it stung! I could not control the pressure of this surging anger and pounced on him like an enraged panther. Next, my friends had to pull me off him.

*Tip: Watch movies and write down facial expressions, movements, actions, gestures of the actors when they are upset, angry, happy, sad, excited. Use these to describe your own characters when you are writing. This is the best way to learn how to SHOW emotion instead of telling it.*

**Example 2:** It was very hot. The sun shone brightly and they were all sweating profusely. They were very thirsty.

**Improved:** The sun was at full blast. Sweat trickled down their necks like hot tea. They were dehydrated and no amount of water could quench their thirst. The unbearable heat gnawed at them, leaving them thirsty for more.

**Example 3:** I love Christmas season and the things associated with it.

**Improved:** The steam from the hot cocoa warmed my face as I sat on my big rocking chair staring at the warm fire. The fresh pine scent of the dazzling Christmas tree filled the room, adding to the holiday cheer. The delicious aroma of vanilla and ginger cookies made my stomach rumble with hunger. I was filled with joy and excitement and I wished the holidays could last forever.

*Next section can be used as an aid to improve your descriptions.*

# Clouds

| Adjective | Verb | Figure of speech | Sentences |
|---|---|---|---|
| • Scattered | • Drifted | • Fluffy like candy floss | • The fluffy and perfect white clouds drifted across the sky like pure cotton balls. |
| • Dense | • Floated | • Perfect white like cotton balls | • The sliver clouds lazily floated across the moonlit sky. |
| • Grey | • Crumpled | • Scattered like a torn veil | • The dark and swollen clouds burst into tears flooding the village. |
| • Puffy | • Fleeted | | |
| • Fleecy | • Glided |  | |
| • Silvery | • Thickened | | |
| • Swollen | | | |
| • Dark | | | |

## Adjective

- Dark
- Thick
- Gloomy
- Sullen
- Ominous
- Infinite
- Motionless
- Limitless
- Serene
- Crimson
- Cloudless
- Moonlit

## Verb

- Blackens
- Glows
- Blazes
- Glitters
- Shimmers

## Figure of speech

- Like a blanket of darkness
- Like a blanket of jewels
- Like an endless canvas of brilliant blue
- Like an unbroken sea of blue

## Sentences

- The cloudless starlit sky glittered and shimmered like a blanket of jewels.
- The dark and sullen sky reflected her gloomy mood.
- The overcast, ominous sky and strong winds gave warning of the hurricane to come.

| Adjective | Verb | Figure of speech | Sentences |
|---|---|---|---|
| • Orange | • Rise / Rose | • Like God's morning star. | • The blazing golden ball, rose like a glorious medallion in the sky. |
| • Red | • Lit | • Like a fiery ball in the sky | • The brilliant golden sun was radiating down, kissing my face. |
| • Gold | • Blaze | • Glowing like a glorious medallion | • The warm and friendly sun glistened gently as the kids played outdoors welcoming the spring. |
| • Amber | • Glittered | | |
| • Crimson | | | • The smiling sun poured out its crimson hues over the azure ocean. |
| • Brilliant | | | |
| • Glorious | | | |
| • Enormous | | | |
| • Blazing | | | |
| • Scorching | | | |
| • Scintillating | | | |

| Adjective | Verb | Figure of speech | Sentences |
|---|---|---|---|
| • Silver | • Glow | • Like a silvery veil | • The silver moon peeped furtively through the thick grey clouds. |
| • Milky | • Shimmer | • Like a loyal star | |
| • Perfect white | • Wane | • Like the God's flashlight | • The milky moon light stretched like a shiny veil over the Earth. |
| • Brilliant | • Shone | | |
| • Luminous | • Wax |  | • The silver moon shone like a new polished coin in the sky. |
| • Crescent | | | |
| • Sickle | | | • The perfect white moon glowed brilliantly in the sky, guiding the night travellers like God's flashlight. |
| • Full | | | |
| • Pale | | | |
| • Dim | | | |
| • Polished | | | |
| • Romantic | | | |

| Adjective | Verb | Figure of speech | Sentences |
|---|---|---|---|
| • Turquoise | • Rumbled | • Shimmering like a jewel | • The merciless sea rumbled and roared as it powerfully threw the ship around. |
| • Emerald | • Danced | • Smooth as silk | |
| • Calm | • Galloped | • Clear like crystal | • The perfectly calm sea scattered the sunlight like a robe of shimmering jewels. |
| • Smooth | • Soared | • Howled like a wild dog | |
| • Enormous | • Churned | • Like an aqua paradise | • The lapping waves of the turquoise sea murmured and hummed a hypnotic tune. |
| • Vast | • Slapped | | |
| • Brutal | • Foamed | | |
| • Fierce | • Thundered | | |
| • Merciless | • Gurgled | | |
| • Roaring | • Lapped | | |
| • Thunderous | | | |
| • Choppy | | | |

| Adjective | Verb | Figure of speech | Sentences |
|---|---|---|---|
| • Majestic | • Stood | • Dense like spidery knots | • The shadowy trees stooped like ghostly figures intently listening to our conversation. |
| • Spectacular | • Swayed | • Roots like enormous tentacles | • The trees had shed their bright red and orange foliage and looked like eerie skeletons. |
| • Magnificent | • Knotted | • Like swaying feathers | • Majestic trees soared high towards the sky and their boughs stretched out to paint the landscape. |
| • Rotting | • Arched | • Stooped like ghostly figures | |
| • Decaying | • Danced | | |
| • Shadowy | • Fluttered | | |
| • Eerie | • Stoop | | |
| • Snow-covered | • Soar | | |

# Mountains

| Adjective | Verb | Figure of speech | Sentences |
|---|---|---|---|
| • Slippery<br>• Rocky<br>• Stony<br>• Treacherous<br>• Enchanting<br>• Majestic<br>• Spectacular<br>• Snow-capped<br>• Volcanic | • Towered<br>• Expand<br>• Inhabit<br>• Soared | • As slippery as a seal<br>• Loomed like phantoms through the mist<br>• Like sleeping giants<br><br> | • The rocky mountain stood tall and proud, holding hundreds of species of flora and fauna.<br>• The spectacular mountains enchanted the tourists with their snow-capped peaks and picturesque beauty.<br>• The majestic mountain soared high like it wanted to kiss the sky. |

## Adjective

- Exotic
- Native
- Predatory
- Marine
- Aquatic
- Nocturnal
- Tropical
- Flightless
- Migratory
- Gregarious

## Verb

- Chirped
- Rustled
- Brood
- Perched
- Pecked

## Figure of speech

- Sang like sirens
- Sang like angels in the cloud
- As regular as an alarm clock
- Building their nest like little worker bees
- Chirping like a chatter box

## Sentences

- The tropical birds soared in the sky, singing like angels.
- The little birds with fierce personalities frightened their enemy by making scary noises with their wings.
- The white aquatic bird swam across the lake as gracefully as an Olympic swimmer.

# City

| Adjective | Verb | Figure of speech | Sentences |
|---|---|---|---|
| • Dull<br>• Enigmatic<br>• Bustling<br>• Charming<br>• Cosmopolitan<br>• Contemporary<br>• Lively<br>• Touristy<br>• Polluted<br>• Romantic<br>• Sophisticated<br>• Timeless<br>• Congested | • Tower<br>• Expand<br>• Inhabit | • As busy as a bee hive<br>• As ancient as the sun<br>• As clean as a whistle<br>• A city that never sleeps | • The city was a contrast of new and old: skyscrapers towered over ancient monuments.<br>• The cobblestone streets, as ancient as the sun, welcomed us to the timeless city and we instantly fell in love with its charm.<br>• The exuberant city, with its mild climate, authentic restaurants, museums, shops and undulating green hills was a feast for all the senses.<br>• At dusk, the city glittered like the milky way. |

| Adjective | Verb | Figure of speech | Sentences |
|---|---|---|---|
| • Crimson<br>• Lingering<br>• Romantic<br>• Golden<br>• Stunning<br>• Sublime<br>• Tropical<br>• Warm<br>• Serene<br>• Mesmerising | • Fade<br>• Fleet<br>• Vanish<br>• Retreat<br>• Darken | • Like a farewell to the passing day<br>• Like sun dipping on a canvas of gentle blue, pink, yellow and orange<br>• Like a candle being extinguished<br> | • At dusk, the sky's hue darkened and the bright yellow turned to red as if it was on fire.<br>• The crimson sun retreated and seemed to fall over the horizon and bow off the face of the earth.<br>• The mesmerising sunset was like a tumult of colours splashed in the sky. |

| Adjective | Verb | Figure of speech | Sentences |
|---|---|---|---|
| <ul><li>Sandy</li><li>Stoney</li><li>Tranquil</li><li>Private</li><li>Idyllic</li><li>Windswept</li><li>Tropical</li><li>Moonlit</li><li>Yellow/Golden</li><li>Sun-baked</li><li>Forlorn</li></ul> | <ul><li>Soothe</li><li>Relax</li><li>Invigorate</li></ul> | <ul><li>The sun sparkled on the water like gleaming jewels</li><li>Hypnotic like a beautiful painting</li><li>Like an open expanse for reflection</li></ul> | <ul><li>The idyllic beach with golden sand, azure water and the aroma of the fish, was the best place in the world!</li><li>The hypotonic waves rolled over the sun-kissed shore and soothed the on-lookers.</li><li>The relentless beating of the waves on the stony beach was like a lullaby and quietened me to a deep state of tranquillity.</li></ul> |

# Desert

## Adjective

- Lonely
- Arid
- Harsh
- Severe
- Barren
- Dry
- Perpetual
- Vast
- Uninterrupted
- Desolate

## Verb

- Boil
- Scorch
- Swelter
- Oppress
- Wilt

## Figure of speech

- Searing sand, scorching sun & sweltering simoom
- Like a vast expanse of amorphous dunes
- Like a dry and parched mouth reaching for water
- Like a golden yellow ocean of fine sand

## Sentences

- The harsh sun scorched the earth leaving nothing but dry desolation.
- The wilted and wounded plants were desperate for hydration.
- The desert felt like a dangerous and an untameable beast.
- Searing sand, scorching sun and sweltering simoom spared none.

# Wind/Thunder

## Adjective

- Strong
- Rumbling
- Forceful
- Gusty
- Menacing
- Incessant
- Distant
- Livid
- Tempestuous

## Verb

- Crash
- Blast
- Explode
- Burst
- Darken
- Bellow
- Barrage

## Figure of speech

- Like raging drums blasting loudly
- Like a cacophony of clashing cymbals
- Like a busy bowling alley with many falling pins
- Like fury of the gods
- As if heavens might split apart

## Sentences

- The sky darkened as the raging rain poured and the thunder roared across the sky.
- The wind raged, and lighting flashed across the charcoal sky as the thunder cried far in the distance.
- Forceful rains barraged the ground below and the wind tore through the trees as the thunder vibrated the surroundings.

## Adjective

- Snowy
- Lonely
- Grey
- Cold/ Chilly
- Biting
- Frigid
- Barren
- Fierce
- Dreary

## Verb

- Freeze
- Numbed
- Fell
- Wither
- Howled

## Figure of speech

- Like a thick untouched blanket of snow
- Like a perpetual and pristine ice-kissed landscape
- Landscape white like an unfinished painting
- White scenery aching for some splash of colour
- Barren trees standing gracefully like ballet dancers

## Sentences

- As the white fluffy snow landed carelessly on the lonely landscape, the thoughts of a snowball fight filled me up with excitement.
- The nascent rays of the sun creeped out, cutting through the numbing cold giving a fleeting hope of warmth.
- Fierce and adamant cold seeped through her heavy jacket, making her yearn for a cup of steaming hot chocolate.

| Adjective | Verb | Figure of speech | Sentences |
|---|---|---|---|
| • Caramel<br>• Windy<br>• Refreshing<br>• Pleasant<br>• Crisp<br>• Brisk<br>• Red/Yellow/Gold | • Comfort<br>• Refresh<br>• Invigorate<br>• Harvest | • Like a grand finale of a successful summer<br><br>• Like the green clothed trees suddenly burst out into a riot of colour<br><br>• Like a garland full of yellow, orange, red and golden leaves<br><br>• Like the leaves waltzing down to join the mosaic on the ground.<br><br>• Sun rises and sets as if on fast-forward | • The golden leaves pirouetting down gracefully in an invisible spiral was a beautiful sight.<br><br>• The best things about autumn are my mum's heavenly apple pie and the cool invigorating breeze.<br><br>• A crisp autumn morning arrived bringing the pleasant and refreshing smells. |

| Adjective | Verb | Figure of speech | Sentences |
|---|---|---|---|
| • Energetic<br>• Spritely<br>• Cheerful<br>• Effervescent<br>• Vivacious<br>• Fecund<br>• Abundant<br>• Lush | • Stimulate<br>• Revitalize<br>• Replenish<br>• Abound | • Like an abundant feast for the butterflies<br>• Like the flowers promising to garland the Earth<br>• The balmy spring breeze whispering in the ears<br>• The landscape splashed with vibrant colours | • The lively baby foals seemed to welcome the spring.<br>• The surrounding carpets of fecund luscious garden gave a sense of new life.<br>• Stalks of new daffodils shimmered in the sun and seemed to garland the field.<br>• The fresh scent of flowers, the balmy congenial breeze, the soft nascent leaves and the joyful carolling of birds, made her feel effervescent. |

| Adjective | Verb | Figure of speech | Sentences |
|---|---|---|---|
| • Fresh<br>• Sun-drenched<br>• Steamy<br>• Dreamy<br>• Breezy<br>• Unrelenting<br>• Blithe<br>• Scintillating | • Sizzle<br>• Blaze<br>• Unwind | • The fiery hot sun that never seem to set<br><br>• The landscape bathed in bright sunlight<br><br>• Hot golden sun burning like an inferno | • The sun was at full blast and I was dripping sweat from head to toe.<br><br>• The scintillating sun was no longer a summertime friend but an oppressive enemy that snapped energy out of everything.<br><br>• The trees, once green and majestic, appeared defeated and desiccated. |

## Elements of a story logically sequenced

Your story is like a jigsaw puzzle with no picture on the box; you must provide all the pieces of the story so the reader can join them together. Ensure your piece of writing is coherent by following this structure:

1. **Opening**
2. **Characters**
3. **Location / Setting**
4. **Problems / Conflicts**
5. **Resolution / Closing**

### Elements of a story explained

1. **Opening**: The opening paragraph/statement is the most important piece of your story and should hook your reader. This section must be written in a way that captivates the reader and makes them want to read on.

2. **Characters**: Visualise the most important and less important characters. List down how they look, what makes them interesting, their personalities, how they interact with others, their likes/dislikes, hopes/fears.

3. **Location / Setting:** Think about the location or setting where your story takes place. This could be one or more locations. Describe what can you see, hear, smell, taste, feel about the place/setting.

4. **Problems / Conflicts**: Think about problems or conflicts that would occur in your writing. Every conflict must have an introduction, a development, a climax, and resolution. Plan the conflict in such a way that you can give it a believable resolution.

5. **Resolution / Closing**: Think about the resolutions and possible outcomes and how to put them on paper. Readers often keep on reading because they want to know how a conflict is going to be resolved. Don't disappoint the readers by leaving unanswered questions while closing your piece of writing.

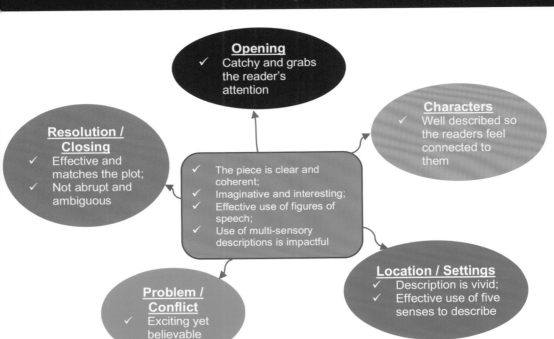

**Opening**
✓ Catchy and grabs the reader's attention

**Characters**
✓ Well described so the readers feel connected to them

**Resolution / Closing**
✓ Effective and matches the plot;
✓ Not abrupt and ambiguous

✓ The piece is clear and coherent;
✓ Imaginative and interesting;
✓ Effective use of figures of speech;
✓ Use of multi-sensory descriptions is impactful

**Problem / Conflict**
✓ Exciting yet believable

**Location / Settings**
✓ Description is vivid;
✓ Effective use of five senses to describe

**The opening of a piece of writing is very important, so always catch the reader's attention by starting with a good opening line. The first few lines set the tone of the story and grab the reader's attention so they wish to read on.**

**There are different ways to start a story, such as:**

1. Starting with an unanswered question intriguing the reader to keep on reading.

2. Starting with a problem or a conflict.

3. Starting with the description of settings.

4. Starting with the description of characters.

5. Starting with a statement or philosophy on life.

6. Starting with an action.

Once upon a time

## Starting with an unanswered question

- *"Whether I shall turn out to be the hero of my own life, or whether that station will be held by anybody else, these pages must show." – David Copperfield by Charles Dickens*

- *"Ever had the feeling your life's been flushed down the toilet?" – The Toilet of Doom by Michael Lawrence*

- Why does trouble always follow me around? Do I have a "kick me" sign on my back or something?

- Have you ever had a day when you wished you had stayed in bed? As I rushed to catch the bus on what seemed to be a perfectly normal day, I had no idea what was ahead of me.

- Have you ever wondered what it would be like to have loads and loads of money? What would you like to spend it on? Your favourite chocolates? Or Ice cream? If Shaon, the kind- hearted, little boy could have even a little money, he would use it to put a smile on the face of his poor, tired mother.

## Starting with a problem or a conflict

- *"When I was four months old, my mother died suddenly and my father was left to look after me all by himself." – Danny the Champion of the World by Roald Dahl.*

- *"I went to sleep with gum in my mouth and now there's gum in my hair and when I got out of bed this morning I tripped on the skateboard and by mistake I dropped my sweater in the sink while the water was running and I could tell it was going to be a terrible, horrible, no good, very bad day." – Alexander and the Terrible, Horrible, No Good, Very Bad Day by Judith Viorst.*

- *"When Denis died, he found himself in another place. Dead people came at him with party hats and presents." — Rachel Swirsky by "Fields of Gold"*

- I was already running late. I had my head down as I neared my class, trying out different excuses to tell the teacher why I was so late. As I was about to go through the classroom door, I saw a quick movement out of the corner of my eye. I felt something hard and wet hit the side of my head, then everything went black.

- If Andy, the kind- hearted, little boy could have even a little money, he would use it to put a smile on the face of his poor, tired mother.

**Starting with a description of a setting**

- 'Far out in the uncharted backwaters of the unfashionable end of the Western Spiral arm of the Galaxy lies a small unregarded yellow sun.' -The Hitchhiker's Guide to the Galaxy by Douglas Adams

- 'In a hole in the ground there lived a hobbit. Not a nasty, dirty, wet hole, filled with the ends of worms and an oozy smell, nor yet a dry, bare, sandy hole with nothing in it to sit down on or to eat: it was a hobbit-hole, and that means comfort.' - The Hobbit by J.R.R. Tolkien

- The hottest day of the summer so far was drawing to a close and a drowsy silence lay over the large, square houses of Privet Drive. – Harry Potter and the Order of the Phoenix by J.K. Rowling

- "It was a dark and stormy night; the rain fell in torrents, except at occasional intervals, when it was checked by a violent gust of wind which swept up the streets (for it is in London that our scene lies), rattling along the house-tops, and fiercely agitating the scanty flame of the lamps that struggled against the darkness…"

## Starting with a description of a character

- *'When he was nearly thirteen, my brother Jem got his arm badly broken at the elbow.' - To Kill A Mockingbird by Harper Lee*

- *"He was an inch, perhaps two, under six feet, powerfully built, and he advanced straight at you with a slight stoop of the shoulders, head forward, and a fixed from-under stare which made you think of a charging bull." – Lord Jim by Joseph Conrad*

- *Once there were four children whose names were Peter, Susan, Edmund and Lucy. – The Lion, the Witch and the Wardrobe by C.S. Lewis*

- *Bob is my little brother, and he's in the first grade. He's fearless. One day, he wore a cape to school. I told him everyone would laugh at him. The next day, five other boys came wearing capes.*

- Dinosaurs walked the earth thousands of years ago. Yes, I know that's what the textbooks say. But have you seen my Mathematics teacher, particularly when he calls over each boy to his table to check the homework notebooks? He looks like a dinosaur out hunting for its next meal. And from the looks of it, I might be his unlucky prey today.

**Starting with a statement or philosophy on life**

- *"A life is made of great number of small incidents and small number of great incidents." – Going Solo by Roald Dahl*

- *"Happy families are all alike; every unhappy family is unhappy in its own way." - Anna Karenina by Leo Tolstoy*

- *"It's a funny thing about mothers and fathers. Even when their own child is the most disgusting little blister you could ever imagine, they still think that he or she is wonderful." – Matilda by Roald Dahl*

- *"It is a truth universally acknowledged that a single man in possession of a good fortune must be in want of a wife." - Pride and Prejudice by Jane Austen*

- A seemingly large problem does not seem so large once something larger comes along.

## Starting with an action

- *"The stranger came early in February, one wintry day, through a biting wind and a driving snow, the last snowfall of the year, over the down, walking as it seemed from Bramblehurst railway station, and carrying a little black portmanteau in his thickly gloved hand."* - The Invisible Man by H.G. Wells

- *"On 24 May 1863, which was a Sunday, my uncle, Professor Lidenbrock, came rushing back towards his little house, No. 19 Königstrasse, one of the oldest streets in the old quarter of Hamburg."* - Journey to the Centre of the Earth by Jules Verne

- "It was seven o'clock of a very warm evening in the Seeonee hills when Father Wolf woke up from his day's rest, scratched himself, yawned, and spread out his paws one after the other to get rid of the sleepy feeling in their tips."- *The Jungle Book* by Rudyard Kipling

- *"Here is Edward Bear, coming down the stairs now, bump bump bump, on the back of his head, behind Christopher Robin."*- Winnie-the-Pooh by A.A. Milne

- I crouched in starting position, hands poised on the track and back coiled like a spring. "On your mark! Get set!" The starting gun boomed. I launched myself forward, trying to spring ahead of the pack.

- As the ground beneath their feet shook, Harry and Ron wondered if it was an earthquake. As the crockery started tumbling out from the cabinets, the boys ran helter and skelter trying to remember the drill they had been taught at school. "Wait a minute!" Ron cried out, "we have to get the baby. He is upstairs in his crib!!!"

**Create different story openings based on this scenario:**

*A school boy is getting ready for school and is worried about what the day may hold.*

*A few suggestions have been given in the following cards. Can you try to make some of your own?*

**Start with a problem or a conflict**

- The headmaster was approaching. Time was running out. I needed to get in quick. The threat of a detention hung like a sword over my head as I hopelessly waited for an opportunity to sneak into the classroom.

- As I ran down the hallway towards my classroom, my foot slipped on a small puddle on the floor. My feet slid out from underneath me, making me fall backwards and sending my books flying in every direction. Soon a considerable audience gathered, adding to my mortification.

**Begin by asking a question to get the reader thinking**

- Have you ever had a day when you wished you had stayed in bed? As I rushed to catch the bus on what seemed to be a perfectly normal day, I had no idea what was ahead of me.

- I was so frustrated that I was late for school. Mum usually wakes me up, but this morning she didn't. She always does, but this morning the house was silent: no note, no car in the drive, no breakfast set out for me, her bed not slept in. Where was my mother?

## Start with the description of a setting(s)

- Freezing cold rain was pelting the back of my head as I ran towards the school, avoiding the mud puddles that were forming in the old, cracked parking lot. There was a chill and smell in the air that reminded me that autumn was right around the corner.

- Realising I was very late for school, I jumped out of my bed and nearly tripped over the heaped pile of dirty clothes next to it. I looked around the messy room for a clean shirt and grabbed the one that was on top of the pile of clothes on the chair next to the door. Making my way out of the room, I ran down the stairs, taking two at a time.

## Start with the description of a character

- My mind raced as I wondered where my mother had gone. She was the one constant in my life. I thought of her dark hair and eyes, eyes that had a constant sparkle in them as if she were about to laugh. She always had a smile or words of encouragement for me.

- I nervously looked down the hallway inside the school building, trying to spot my best friend. He was always so easy to spot. He had a head full of bright red hair that refused to ever be completely combed. A few strands of hair would always be sticking up.

## Begin with an interesting fact or a statement

- Shock has been known to kill school kids. It can cause their brains to explode and their hearts to stop dead still. These facts raced through my mind, as I stood dumbfounded in front of my year five classmates. I wish I had stayed in bed!

- True friendship is tested when one's pride is hurt.

- My day today was like a game of dominos: once one thing happened, so many others followed in sequence.

- There are bad days and then there are worse days.

## Begin with an action

- "Buzzzzzz!" The sound of my alarm clock droned in my ears and with a startle, I sat straight up in my bed. This was my big day, and I had to be on time.

- The heavy classroom door swung shut with a loud "bang!" As if in unison, the whole class turned their heads sharply to the right. There I stood in front of everyone. So much for sneaking in quietly.

A good author can bring characters in a story to life. The characters speak to the reader, steer the plot, set the theme, and create emotions in a story.

Character traits are aspects of a person's behaviour and personality. Character traits are revealed through the characters' response to a conflict through dialogue and descriptions.

Outlining traits like appearance, education, influences, hopes, fears, ambitions, hobbies of the characters makes the reader feel connected to them.

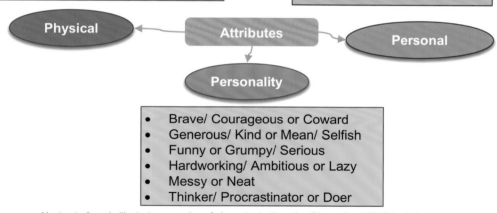

- Age
- Gender
- Voice
- Height/Built
- Assets/ Strengths
- Flaws
- Colour/ Texture of the skin/hair

- Family
- Wealth/ Possessions
- Lifestyle
- Friends/ Colleagues
- Hobbies
- Beliefs
- Profession

**Physical** ← **Attributes** → **Personal**

**Personality**

- Brave/ Courageous or Coward
- Generous/ Kind or Mean/ Selfish
- Funny or Grumpy/ Serious
- Hardworking/ Ambitious or Lazy
- Messy or Neat
- Thinker/ Procrastinator or Doer

*Next set of cards illustrate examples of character traits using **Show, Don't Tell** technique.*

**Neat**

1. She looked flawless with her stylish tight bun.

2. Her silk gown and hair neatly held back with a diamond headband made her look like a princess.

3. Her hair was soft, silky and long like Rapunzel.

4. The gorgeous dark brown curls foamed luxuriously over her shoulders.

5. Her hair was sprucely braided like a thick black rope.

6. She looked flawless with her wavy red hair.

7. Voluminous coffee brown hair with creamy caramel highlights looked irresistible on her.

8. Her dramatic curls gracefully swept to one side.

9. Lovely dark hair spiced with reddish streaks looked perfect with her skin tone.

**Unkempt**

1. His unruly orange hair fell into his eyes.

2. Her rough chestnut curls cascaded down her back.

3. A shaggy mane covered her eyes.

4. Her hair was like black steel wool.

5. The bangs that obscured his eyes reminded me of a sheepdog.

6. His hair was flaked with snowy dandruff.

7. The long spiky hair looked as if he had put his finger in a light socket.

8. Her choppy hair was chemically damaged.

**Bald**

1. His scalp gleamed like a full moon.
2. His hair was rapidly receding at the temples.
3. His barren scalp reminded him of the faded glory he once enjoyed.
4. His hair barely covered his scalp.
5. Fluorescent lights reflected off his scalp.
6. At the first sight of baldness he got his hair shaved off like a soldier and he looked better.
7. Her hair was fighting a stubborn fight against baldness.
8. His huge, smooth, bare head made him look like an alien.
9. The baldness exaggerated the shape of his head.

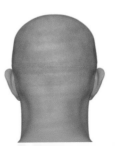

**Old**

1. Her grandma's hair was as white as a cotton wool.

2. Although he felt like twenty, the streaked lines of pure white hair gave his age away.

3. Sagging skin, creaking joints, grizzled hair, blurring eyes and fading memories made her realise time is a thief stealing away everything she had.

4. Powder-white hair and craggy pale skin reflected his age.

5. The neat salt-and-pepper hair looked graceful.

6. Her hair once shiny black was now smoky-grey; her memories, once sharp, were now disappearing.

7. Her hair, once shimmering black are now just frilly white.

**Sad**

1. Her puffy and tired eyes demanded rest.

2. Her damp eyes gave away her story.

3. The news glazed her eyes with a layer of tears.

4. As she blinked, tears trickled down from her eyelids.

5. Her eyes suddenly swam with tears.

6. His tears burst out like water from a dam.

7. His eyes were swollen and red from weeping.

8. The fire in his eyes was replaced by profound sadness.

9. His eyes cast down in a mournful gaze after he heard his test results.

10. Her eyes tinged with sadness as she gazed on some faraway spot.

11. His pale yellow eyes spoke volumes about his illness.

12. The traveller's sunken eyes spoke of days of hunger.

13. She looked at the rain with unseeing eyes filled with the visions of the past.

**Happy**

1. Her hazel eyes danced with laughter.
2. Her pearly eyes sparkled impishly.
3. Her eyes lit like candles in the dark.
4. Her gentle stare filled us with hope.
5. Her eyes shone like sparkling emeralds.
6. Her beady eyes gleamed with joy and pride.

7. Her mesmerizing eyes softened with love.
8. Tears of joy rolled down her cheeks.
9. Her friendly and warm eyes made us comfortable.
10. Her lively eyes illuminated the room.

**Angry / Alert**

1. Her eyes burnt with anger.
2. His piercing grey eyes turned red with anger.
3. His bloodshot eyes burnt with cruelty.
4. The constables' hawk eyes drilled through their pretence.

5. He found himself being stared at threateningly by the attacker.
6. Her eyes squinted as she evaluated the danger round her.
7. Her eyes narrowed in defiance and a fierce look marked her face.
8. Archie couldn't escape the watchful eyes of the teacher.
9. Finding his arch nemesis in front of him so unexpectedly, Harry's eyes narrowed into slits.

**Excited / Happy**

1. She flashed her beaming smile to the audience.
2. Her face glowed with happiness.
3. Her whole body shivered with excitement.
4. His laughter echoed in the room.
5. As soon as she heard the news, she leapt in the air with excitement.
6. The children couldn't control their giggles.
7. Her face broke into a wide grin
8. She was bubbling with a smile.
9. Enthusiasm shone on her face.
10. Her smile was like a ray of sunshine
11. She couldn't hide her impish grin.
12. There was a bounce in his step and he was whistling a happy tune.

**Scared**

1. Still trembling, he wiped the sweat from his brow.
2. His heart shuddered when he realised he had stumbled over a carcass.
3. A sudden urge to flee overtook her.
4. She froze and her muscles tightened.
5. Her mouth felt dry and her head was dizzy.
6. The colour drained from her face and she took small steps backwards.
7. The fear paralyzed him.
8. My heart began to hammer against my chest.
9. His stomach was in knots and his breath quickened.
10. Fear clutched her throat and she couldn't even shout for help even though she was desperate for it!
11. A tremor of dread slid through her, leaving her all shaken.

**Sad**

1. He was dominated by profound sadness.
2. Her face looked as if holding a thousand ocean of tears.
3. He felt an achy hollowness.
4. Her bottom lip quivered while she cried.
5. Cold and unending sorrow overpowered him.
6. Her smile looked fake, only a mask to hide the hollow achy heart.
7. She bit her lip to stop the tears from rolling out.
8. Her breathy gasps reverberated around the room.
9. Her anguished face was a window to her bereaved heart.

**Strict/Angry**

1. His teacher had a hawkish aura about her and every time she entered the classroom the noises dimmed and kids sat up with alertness.

2. He was learning about a ruthless dictator in their history lesson and all he could think of was his own father.

3. As he slammed the door behind him, his face was red like brick, eyes as if they would pop out, and he was moving his hands wildly like flies in a fruit jar.

4. Anyone who was ever around him instantly felt uncomfortable because of his glinting, narrowed eyes and the permanent scowl etched on his face.

5. As the headmaster walked down the hall, a wake of silence followed him, and students instantly stood up straight.

**Positive**

1. She did not have laser eyes, nor could she read minds, but she was their superhero and they felt truly motivated.

2. Her dim blue eyes shone with warmth and her friends and family always felt safe expressing their thoughts and feelings to her.

3. She was thoughtful, accessible and caring and never too busy to listen to people who needed her.

4. He was not just a father but a true leader; he always encouraged his kids to see rocks in their paths as opportunities to work harder.

5. He never undermined anyone's feelings or opinions and always had a wonderful way of giving feedback with a style of humour they could relate to.

6. She is funny and intelligent, and always wins the war of linguistic acrobatics with her witty retorts.

7. He knows how to look on the brighter side and is always happy.

8. She is a meticulous person who plans, thinks, strategizes and prepares in advance; no wonder success is just a habit for her.

**Hardworking**

1. Sweat streamed down the side of his flushed face as he struggled to finish mowing the lawn on the hot, summer day.

2. People knew that they could count on him to keep his word, no matter what it took to finish the task.

3. Fingers flying over the keyboard, she continued writing her homework report even though her friends were in the other room laughing and playing.

4. Even though everyone else had given up and gone home for the night, she continued to clean the counters and table tops as instructed.

5. He was the only one graduating from his class of fifty students who actually finished college and got a degree.

**Lazy / careless**

1. He ate junk food, drank alcohol and treated people like they have an expiry date. He never grew up or took responsibility of his life.

2. She moved as slowly as possible in hopes that by the time she reached the party room, all of the cleaning up had been taken care of already.

3. Piles of clothes, candy bar wrappers, and toys were scattered all over every inch of the floor around him as he hypnotically stared at the TV.

4. He spent more time making excuses and arguing about why he could not do his chores than it would have taken him to just do the jobs in the first place.

5. She would rather go buy disposables than go through the tedious chore of washing dishes.

*The Adventures of Huckleberry Finn by Mark Twain*

- He was most fifty, and he looked it. His hair was long and tangled and greasy, and hung down, and you could see his eyes shining through like he was behind vines. It was all black, no grey; so was his long, mixed-up whiskers. There wasn't no colour in his face, where his face showed; it was white; not like another man's white, but a white to make a body sick, a white to make a body's flesh crawl – a tree-toad white, a fish-belly white. As for his clothes – just rags, that was all. He had one ankle resting on the other knee; the boot on that foot was busted, and two of his toes stuck through, and he worked them now and then. His hat was laying on the floor – an old black slouch with the top caved in, like a lid.

*The Black Cauldron by Lloyd Alexander*

- A bellow of laughter resounded beyond the chamber, and in another moment a giant, red- headed warrior rolled in at the side of Adaon. He towered above all in the chamber and his beard flamed around a face so scarred with old wounds it was impossible to tell where one began and another ended. His nose had been battered to his cheekbones; his heavy forehead was nearly lost in a fierce tangle of eyebrows; and his neck seemed as thick as Taran's waist.

*Look Homeward, Angel by Thomas Wolfe*

- My brother Ben's face, thought Eugene, is like a piece of slightly yellow ivory; his high white head is knotted fiercely by his old man's scowl; his mouth is like a knife, his smile the flicker of light across a blade. His face is like a blade, and a knife, and a flicker of light: it is delicate and fierce, and scowls beautifully forever, and when he fastens his hard white fingers and his scowling eyes upon a thing he wants to fix, he sniffs with sharp and private concentration through his long, pointed nose...his hair shines like that of a young boy—it is crinkled and crisp as lettuce.

*A Separate Peace by John Knowles*

- For such an extraordinary athlete—even as a Lower Middler Phineas had been the best athlete in the school—he was not spectacularly built. He was my height—five feet eight and a half inches...He weighed a hundred and fifty pounds, a galling ten pounds more than I did, which flowed from his legs to torso around shoulders to arms and full strong neck in an uninterrupted, unemphatic unity of strength.

- List 5 names from people in your friends and family. List down positive and/or negative character traits for each.

- List 5 superheroes / villains from your favourite movies or books or real-life heroes in your life or from history. Do a similar exercise as above for these characters too.

- Here are some examples:

| Person | Character Vocabulary |
|--------|----------------------|
| Steve Jobs | charismatic, passionate, innovator, enterprising, resilient, perfectionist, visionary, narcissist |
| Winston Churchill | charismatic leader, passionate, visionary, courageous, indomitable, astute, resolute, self-assured |
| Helen Keller | courageous, indomitable, resilient, determined, undaunted |
| Mahatma Gandhi | truthful, steadfast, sublime, resilient, selfless, charismatic leader, poised, simple, strong-willed, unperturbed, fearless, |
| Cat in the hat | bungling, clumsy, clownish, creative, goofy, laughable, oafish, scatter-brained, sloppy, uncouth |

Describing a place lucidly is a vital skill to engage the reader. When you visit a location, you experience that place with all your senses. Simple strategy to improve your description of a location or a setting will be to write at a multi-sensory level so the reader is fully immersed and feels that he is actually there.

Describe what the character sees, hears, smells, tastes, and feels to make your descriptions realistic.

Next section can be used as an aid to describe locations vividly.

| **VISION** | **HEARING** | **SMELL** | **TASTE** | **TOUCH** |
|---|---|---|---|---|
|  |  |  |  |  |

**See**

- The sun blazed down from the clear, blue sky to warm the grass under my bare feet.

- I sat down on a bench and took in the surroundings - children playing on the colourful swings while parents kept a watchful eye, the bouncing puppy on a leash next to his owner, and the sweet, older couple walking hand-in-hand down one of the paths.

- The park was laid by broad maples and tall sycamores, providing shade for those tired from their day in the sun.

- Lined by fragrant flower hedges and bushes, the park provided a feast for the butterflies and bees.

- The park on top of the hill was lined by thick, vibrant flower beds, making it look like a paradise against the dry, stark back drop of the desert.

- Straight, gravelled pathways lined by magnificent oak trees wound through the park.

- Through the shade of the oaks, I could see a family of squirrels merrily chasing each other.

**Smell**

- As I sat under the shade of the trees, the warm scent of honeysuckle wafted through the air.

- The aroma of barbequed food made my stomach growl.

- I took a deep breath as I inhaled the sweet fragrance of flowers in the air.

- The cool air was the perfect blend of sweet lavender and orange blossoms.

- The breeze carried the warm, sweet smell of crushed rosemary leaves that had been trampled under feet.

- The slight hint of freshly-mown grass hung in the background behind all the scents of flowers.

- The cidery smell of apples on the ground made me feel hungry.

**Feel/Emotions**

- I wondered what it would be like under the shade of the oaks instead of on the hot, metal park bench.

- In the shade of the oaks the dew-covered grass under my feet energised me.

- As I laid down on the ground and felt the cool, soft grass under my hands, a sense of relaxation overtook me.

- I could feel a gentle breeze on my face, giving relief from the hot sun.

**Hear**

- The symphony of birds singing, the humming of the bees, and laughter of frolicking children made me feel effervescent.

- A high-pitched, squeaky playground gate cut through the pleasantness of the relaxing atmosphere, grating on my nerves.

- I smiled at the noise of the dogs barking as they chased one another, reminding me of my own little dog waiting at home.

- Mothers tried to shush crying babies at the playground.

- As the sun started to go down for the evening, the gentle hum of crickets began to soothe me.

- Mothers called their children, telling them it was time to go home for the day.

**See**

- A kaleidoscope of vibrant corals under water created a feast for the divers' eyes.

- The unbelievably clear beach, clean water with hundreds of shades of blues and greens, along with white sugar sand beaches was a photographer's dream.

- The pristine beach with its calm turquoise waters and the coral reefs was a truce spectacle to witness.

- The water was so brilliantly blue that it made the sky look pale.

- The beach, with crystal clear and warm waters, shade, sun, and powder white sand, never seemed to end.

- The beauty of the white sand paradise was accented by clear water and colourful fishing boats.

- The blue and brown glass pebbles that covered the beach were a sight to behold.

**Feel**

- She could feel the soft sand beneath her feet, still damp from the retreating tide.

- I stood still facing the warm breeze to soak it all in.

- As the sand trickled through my fingers, I was filled with excitement as the thought of holiday had sunk in.

- As I saw the dolphins frolicking in the water, excitement rose up my throat making me scream for joy.

**Smell**

- The fresh sea breezes filled my nostrils, lifting the atmosphere.
- The air was heavy with the mist from the waves spraying in the air.
- The briny aroma mixed with the fragrance of the fishing fleet rose up to meet my nostrils.
- As she relaxed on the golden beach, a hint of sunscreen filled her nostrils

**Hear**

- I could hear the crashing of the waves and the faint sound of birds in the background.
- Against the percussion of the waves was the laughter; coming in bursts and rolling like the ocean.
- As I walked, pebbles crunched beneath my boots and the waves lapped in their steady rhythm.
- The sound of water dragging numerous rounded stones up and down the beach added to the splendour of the moment.
- Occasionally a few seagulls squawked as they cautiously looked for any food dropped by the travellers.

**See**

- The whole area is untouched: no stores, no restaurants, just nature at its best.

- The heavenly view seemed like a mirage and was photographer's dream.

- A place in the sun that warrants returning again and again.

- The habitat was bursting with thousands of tropical plants and animals.

- Situated in the pristine scenery of the Alps with stunning mountain views in every direction, it was heavenly.

- The spectacular magnificence of the snow-capped peak was like nature's ornament.

- Driving a route through the magical canyons shaped by migrating glaciers thousands of years ago was just surreal.

- The peak of the mountain offered spectacular views of the vibrant city.

- The mineral in the water gave it an elegant emerald colour.

- The peak was a unique combination of ruthlessly rugged terrain and sublime beauty.

**Emotions**

- A thirst for adventure and beauty overtook her as she climbed the tallest peak.

- I felt like I was flying with the breeze gently washing over my face.

- I was awe-stuck and my eyes didn't know how to blink at that moment.

- I was buzzing with excitement as the beauty of the place overtook me.

- She was so engrossed in the beauty of the place that it made her aches and pains vanish.

- A lovely place where I could go with my sketching pad and draw until the light drained from the sky.

- I left with a feeling that I had to come back again.

**Smell**

- The sweet smell of flowers cut through the soft scent of the morning's dewy grass.

- The smell of rain bearing winds filled my nostrils.

- The cidery smell of apples on the ground made me feel hungry.

- The exciting smell of the blooming hills was very refreshing.

- The smell of fresh morning dew was enough to wake me up.

- The sweet fragrance of lavender surrounded them.

**Hear**

- The waterfall thundered as it gushed down like a beam of light.

- Twittering of birds, gossiping while they perched on the tall trees.

- We could hear the flapping of wings of a great blue heron as it soared over the murmuring creek.

See

- Like a scene from an old horror movie; I looked down a narrow alley and saw a ghostly silhouette of a rundown factory in the distance.

- The windows were broken and there was a huge hole in the roof.

- It was overcrowded by hostile thorn bushes and vines that climbed like snakes up the walls.

- As I approached the front of the building, I followed a long, untrodden passageway into the darkness.

- The crumbling walls encircled me as if I were the victim of an ambush.

- I peered nervously through the darkness, seeing looming shapes everywhere.

- As I entered what had been a large assembly line factory, I saw rusted tools which appeared to have become one with the damp soil, and scraps of bent metal lay scattered on the floor.

- Spiders had laced the walls and doorways with their webs; stretched like pieces of art across my path.

- In the main entrance hung a huge rusted door, clinging on by just one remaining hinge.

Emotions / Feelings

- Something drew me towards the abandoned building; it was like an invisible hand was pulling me closer and closer to it.

- As I cut my way through the dense fog and entered the dilapidated building, shivers immediately ran down my spine.

- I couldn't help the wild thoughts that churned in my mind. Why had this place been abandoned? Had some horrible tragedy happened here?

- As I passed through a narrow doorway, spider webs clung to my face, which I unsuccessfully tried to brush away.

- A thick, dense fog hung over the whole building and I found it hard to breath in air heavy with moisture.

- A heavy depression fell on me and I knew I wouldn't be coming back to this place ever again.

- As distance between myself and the old building grew, I could feel myself starting to relax again.

- The squeaking and scratching of the hundreds of fleeing rats made me nauseous.

**Hear**

- As I walked down the narrow alley towards the dilapidated building, the constant noise of the busy city slowly faded away and became only distant echoes.

- As I stood in front of the crumbling building, nothing stirred; there was only an eerie silence.

- A long and a slow screech split the silence as I pulled the old, rusted door open.

- Loose gravel crunched under my sneakers as I tried to run away from the abandoned house.

- As I entered the main factory floor, all I could hear was the constant trickle of water coming in from the holes in the roof.

- As I entered the room, all I could hear was a faint scratching.

- The squeaking and scratching of the terrified rats made me realize that I had disturbed a huge rats' nest.

**Smell**

- As I neared the dilapidated factory building, the pungent smell of rotting garbage from the alleyway burned my nostrils.

- Even the windows seemed to frown from the dank and humid smell of the building.

- The smell of something rotting rose up, and the sickness of the smell almost paralyzed me.

- As rats scurried out from under my feet, I could clearly see that the pungent smell was from several decaying rodents lying on the floor.

- I immediately turned around and fled that horrible room and that sickening smell quickly cleared from my nose.

- I entered the main room and heavy dust clogged my nostrils and lungs.

**See**

- I entered the lush, green jungle through a thick blanket of palm fronds.
- The forest was alive and bursting with activity: birds darted in and out the foliage, monkeys swung and played in the tops of the trees, and small animals scurried through the underbrush.
- A line of palm trees reached towards the sky like a majestic crowd of vivid green umbrellas.
- As I passed through the dense foliage, light and shadow danced across my skin.
- The path suddenly grew dark and as I looked up through the tree tops it felt as if the ghostly stooped figures were staring down at me.
- The wind made the trees lash and crash against each other.
- I saw steam rise up from the plant leaves as the bright sun quickly dried the rain.

**Feelings / Emotions**

- I felt a surge of pure joy as I looked around the colourful jungle surrounding me.

- I wondered how many humans besides me had ever entered this part of the forest.

- The rough bark of trees and the soft petals of flowers were such a contrast to each other under my fingers.

- I felt a sudden cold breeze and looked up to see heavy storm clouds forming above me.

- Almost immediately, heavy raindrops began filtering through the dense foliage and splashed on my upturned face.

- The darkness of the clouds above me created a sense of urgency in me to retreat back to the safety of my hut.

- As I vigilantly moved through the dense jungle, it was hard to avoid the branches caressing me and the cobwebs brushing my pale skin.

**Smell**

- The sweet smell of tropical flowers floated on the warm breeze.
- The deeper and deeper I got into the jungle, a strong and earthy aroma surrounded me.
- I could smell a slight hint of honey and beeswax as I anxiously passed a bee hive alongside the trail.
- The jungle smelled better than any greenhouse ever could – the slight smell of moist dirt and leaves, accented with the slightest hint of jasmine.
- I could sense a sudden change in the air; it smelt like rain was coming.
- The unique and unforgettable odour of decaying leaves, moist earth and damp wood overtook me.
- Fresh resinous smell of the pine was very refreshing.
- The musky coniferous odours were penetrating and unforgettable.

**Hear**

- The faint sound of rustling foliage gave me a bit of a fright of what could be approaching.
- I could hear the faint sound of a waterfall in the distance.
- I smiled as I heard the chatter of monkeys and watched them swing and play in the tree branches high above me.
- The entire jungle suddenly grew silent: nothing stirred; nothing sang.
- I heard a few splatters of raindrops on the dense foliage around me.
- The wind wailed around me as I ran for cover from the heavy rain.
- All we could hear was the cracking sound of dry leaves as we walked.

**See**

- The insipid and neglected hallway was crammed with patients on trolleys, some tended by strained relatives and some alone.

- The floor was shining clean with long corridors and polystyrene tiled ceiling. The waiting room was large, rectangular, well-lit and buzzing with people.

- The aisles were busy with patients in wheel chairs wearing their hospital gowns.

- Above the double doors were the large banal plastic sign, dark with white lettering.

- The nurses and doctors hurried from room to room on their rounds.

- The Ivory walls were scraped in places from the hundreds of trolleys that have bumped into them.

- The wide entrance of A&E had automatic sliding glass doors; ambulances lined up outside, paramedics wheeling in patients on trollies.

- The waiting area had a television and plastic chairs; it was as comfortable as a train station.

**Emotion**

- The rapid heartbeat calmed and her face relaxed after seeing the report.
- As she listened to the nurse, a troubled expression settled on her face.
- She felt edgy and nervous.
- Her stomach gripped with anxiety as she waited in the hallway.
- It was as if a massive truckload lifted when they found the disease is curable.
- I shivered anxiously in the claustrophobic cubicle and waited for the signal.

**Smell**

- The air was heavy with stifling antiseptic smell.
- The air was pungent with the strong odour of disinfectant.
- The strong, antiseptic smell reeked of the unpleasant possibilities of this place.
- The hospital corridor was stuffy and the air had an undertone of bleach.

**Hear**

- The confined space magnified the groans and wails of the patients.
- The wheels of the stretcher and my pounding footsteps were the only things I could hear.
- The steady beeping of the medical equipment was masked by the shrieks of the patients.

**See**

- A storm cloud suddenly blocked the sunshine, and she involuntarily shivered.
- The sea had been as smooth as a pane of glass, but waves formed seemingly out of nowhere and rose higher and higher.
- Suddenly it was a battle between the air and the sea as the harsh winds attacked the waves and hammered the ship.
- She jumped up off her chair and ran for cover, along with scores of other confused travellers.
- A jagged bolt of lightning tore through the pitch-black sky, briefly illuminating the raging sea.
- She could see seagulls scattering in all directions, trying to find shelter from the storm.
- The uprooted palm tree, tossed on the beach, divulged the story of storm that had passed.
- The wind made the trees lash and crash against each other.

**Hear**

- The background noises drowned in the sound of brutal waves lapping up against the side of the cruise ship.

- She was brought back to reality by the faint clap of thunder far in the distance.

- At first, she heard just a few drops of rain here or there that fell on the deck beside her chair; but then in an instant it became violent and loud, tearing down everything in its way.

- The rain fell so heavily that it nearly deafened her.

- She closed her room door behind her with a loud bang; she was finally safe.

**Smell**

- There was a sudden change in the atmosphere; maybe it was the added salt in the air.

- The sharp, pungent smell was a little alarming.

- The salt-laden air seemed to overwhelm her senses and drowned the lingering smell that came from the pool.

**Emotions / Feelings**

- It was a war between the air and the water, and she felt caught between them.

- As she ran for cover, she tried to grab the railing but the spray from the crashing waves had made it slick, and her hand slipped.

- Fear gripped her heart as she slipped and fell on the rough wooden deck.

- She felt a searing pain as she skinned her knee on the deck while rushing to the shelter.

- The charcoal sky and torrential rains made her heart shudder.

- Almost immediately, heavy needle like raindrops began filtering through the dense foliage and splashed on my upturned face.

- The darkness of the clouds above created a sense of urgency in me to retreat back to the safety of my hut.

- I felt a sudden cold breeze and looked up to see heavy storm clouds forming above me.

**See**

- The sky was nearly cloudless, bathing the field in the gentle moonlight.

- It felt like hundreds of lightning bugs glowed and blinked all around me.

- I looked around me and the twinkling of the lightning bugs made the field seem as if it were wearing a sequined cloak.

- The stars sprinkled the night sky like silver snowflakes.

- Along the edge of the bordering forest, I could see a pair of yellow, glowing eyes staring at me through the darkness.

- A jagged bolt of lightning tore through the pitch-black sky, briefly illuminating it.

- Through the dark field, I could see the shadows of the towering sunflowers waving in the gentle summer breeze.

- It was like a pitch-black curtain draped the sky; the moon was casting luminous shadows on the world below.

- The clouds drowned the sliver glow of the moon and all we could see was ominous black.

**Feelings**

- The crisp night breeze gently caressed my face as I walked through the darkened field.

- I felt the brush of the blades of grass against my legs as I walked through the knee-high wheat field.

- I wondered how it would feel to sleep under the open sky on such a beautiful night like this.

- A sense of peace washed over me as I strolled through the dark open field and all my fears seemed to vanish into the night.

- A sudden nervousness gripped my stomach as I saw a pair yellow, glowing eyes getting closer and closer to me.

- I wondered what small creatures could be hiding beneath my feet as I walked through the unknown darkness.

- The dark and threatening night was ominous black and I felt as if I was surrounded by silent sleeping souls.

**Smell**

- Coming from a nearby yard, I could smell freshly-mowed grass on the breeze.
- There was a sweet, intoxicating perfume hanging in the air from the cluster of butterfly bushes alongside the field.
- I deeply inhaled the fresh, clean air.
- I could tell someone nearby was having a campfire; I could faintly smell the burning pine logs.
- Wild roses were in full bloom, filling the air with their sweet fragrance.
- The smell of fresh green leaves filtered through the other smells of the summer night.

**Hear**

- I could hear the swaying wheat as the stalks brushed up against each other.
- As the night progressed, all the sounds had faded and the only thing you could hear was the flapping of the sheets on the clothes' line in the backyard.
- Off in the distance was the occasional hoot of a lone owl breaking the tranquillity of the night.
- The crickets provided a peaceful choir for me as I strolled through the field.
- A rustling of leaves drew my attention to the edge of the field that was bordering the forest.
- The sound of light footsteps grew closer and closer.
- A jagged bolt of lightning tore through the peaceful night.
- A rustling in some nearby foliage made me hold my breath and wonder: what wild animal was out there, hunting me down?

**See**

- I looked down from the hilltop onto the land below and the sandy white beach was littered with sea shells; I could see the outline of coral underneath the crystal-clear water.

- The picturesque view almost made me forget that I was stranded on this island.

- Gentle waves lapped at the beach, washing up strands of seaweed.

- The thick, green jungle growth was the picture of tranquillity, but it hid the fact that it was crawling with poisonous snakes and dangerous pitfalls.

- For as far as my eyes could see, my island was the only one in sight.

- Nothing broke up the flat landscape of the sea; it seemed to go on forever.

- I headed down the steep, rocky trail, huge boulders stood in my way at nearly every turn.

- I stopped and scanned the area for any potential hazards, only to see a tiny bird hopping out of the bush.

- The uprooted palm tree, tossed on the beach, divulged the story of a storm that had passed.

**Smell**

- Normally I would have thought the sea air refreshing but knowing that it was what separated me from my loved ones, all I could seem to focus on was the smell of decaying fish.

- The smells of bananas and papayas filled my nostrils, overwhelming me with hunger as I stood at the edge of the thick forest.

- I was able to crack open a fallen coconut and the light scent of its milk calmed me as I drank deeply.

- A thick, unidentified odour hung in the air, making me nervous.

- The water smelled of moist dirt and decaying leaves; I couldn't decide if I liked the smell or not.

**Emotion**

- Fear began to rise up in my throat as I realized that I was completely alone on this island.

- I knew I would have to find drinkable water soon; my throat was horribly dried and parched.

- My soaked and weary limbs shivered with fear despite the warm sunshine above.

- I had sustained several cuts on my arms and legs during the crash and the deepest wounds began to throb heavily.

- I knew I would have to fight to survive on this beautiful, yet secluded island.

- My heart grew heavy as I mourned the loss of friends from the crash.

- Hunger made my stomach growl and brought me back to reality; I needed food and fresh drinking water more than anything.

**Hear**

- The lapping of the waves on the beach was a constant backdrop as I stood at the edge of the ocean, deep in thought.

- A fish splashed somewhere nearby, making me hungry for dinner.

- As I was overcome by thirst, I headed into the jungle towards the slightest sound of running water.

- The palm trees creaked and swayed in the gentle ocean breeze.

- The absolute silence on the island was intimidating.

- I held my breath as I heard rustling in some nearby foliage; my heart raced: what or who could be there?

The elements of a story can be broadly categorised into: conflict, action and resolution. The character is faced with a problem (conflict) that they must struggle to overcome (action), and they either win or lose (resolution).

A conflict can either be a generic one, such as good vs. evil. Or it can be man vs. nature, or man vs. community or society or sometimes even an internal conflict of man vs. self. It sets the stage for the rest of the plot, and lets the reader know why they should care about the characters in your story.

Without a conflict, characters will have nothing to grapple with and your story will be boring.

Conflict forces characters to act and reveal who they are. When the conflict exposes who the character really is, the reader feels connected to them.

Make your conflict exciting yet believable. Ensure you can resolve it. Never end with, "it was all a dream"!

## Character Vs. Character

The main character or the protagonist can face conflict from an antagonist. The conflict can be physical fight or can be in the form of a competition or a race.

Such as in Harry Potter a conflict between Lord Voldemort and *Harry potter*.

## Character Vs. Nature

The character is in conflict with nature. Such a as a character fighting against a natural disaster, or a living animal, or a fight against a disease and so on. In 'Running Wild' by Michael Morpurgo, the environmental factors pose a challenge to a boy's survival in the Indonesian jungle after being saved from a tsunami by an elephant.

## Character vs. Self

The character has an internal conflict. Such as, a character is struggling to take a decision whether to go or not to go, or to pursue a path or nor or just trying to find out the best option and so on. In the book 'Call of the Wild' by Jack London, the protagonist (in this case, a dog) is torn between a domesticated self and wild self.

The book 'Crime and Punishment' by Fyodor Dostoyevsky focuses on the mental anguish and moral dilemmas of Rodion Raskolnikov, an impoverished ex-student in St. Petersburg.

### Character vs. Machine

A conflict between the character and any technology. Such as, fight with a robot or a character trying to keep afloat in a sinking boat, the character trying to fix a broken cell phone in an emergency situation and so on. The book *"2001: A Space Odyssey"* by Arthur C. Clarke, shows the struggle between an astronaut and the super-intelligent computer HAL 9000.

### Character vs. Society

The character is in conflict with the society. Such as a protest against an unjust system, prejudice, oppression and so on. In the book *'Catching Fire'* by Suzanne Collins, rebellion against the tyrannical dictatorship (government) by the protagonist is the main conflict of the story.

In the book *'Animal Farm'* by George Orwell, even though the characters are animals rather than people, it still illustrates a story driven by rebellion against a society. The characters struggle against a corrupt structure to create a new society and continue to experience struggles within the new society.

**Make the Conflict emotional:** Make the conflict mean something for the main character. The readers will be able to relate to it if it means something to the characters. For example, *'The Fault in Our Stars'* by John Green tells the story of a young girl fighting cancer. It is heart-breaking yet brilliantly explores the funny, thrilling, and tragic side of life.

**Make it exciting yet believable:** Ensure that your conflict is realistic and plausible to the genre, world and plot you have created in your story. For example, if you are writing science fiction then use scientific facts as well as fictional ones.

**Add life-threatening and exciting obstacles:** Increase the stakes and show that in order to win, the characters will have to lose something or someone. For example, *'Cirque du Freak'* by Darren Shan is the dark and thrilling story of an ordinary schoolboy entangled into the vampire world. The turn of the events brings him to a threshold where his life is under threat.

**Add time pressure:** Adding time pressure to your conflict raises the pace and tension in your story. For example, *'Point Blank'* by Anthony Horowitz, a fast-paced story about teenage spy Alex, sent by MI6 to infiltrate the exclusive Point Blanc Academy where time is a crucial factor for his mission's success.

The ending to a piece of fiction can make or break your story. Avoid abrupt and stereotypical endings such as he woke up and it was all a dream. When planning your story, you should make sure the ending is effective and connects to the earlier events in the plot.

1. **Resolved Ending:** Resolve the main conflict you have been writing about. End with some final action that brings an end to the conflict conclusively. Any unanswered questions posed in the story must be answered. All loose ends must be tied up. As in the famous fairy-tale Cinderella:

*Cinderella marries the Prince, and they live happily ever after.*

2. **Lesson or Moral Ending:** The main character in the story grows or learns something or changes for better in the end of the story.

*"That was the last time I would ever lie to my friend; the lesson has been learnt."*

*"We all lose battles in life but we can win the war. There is always hope."*

3. **Surprise or Shocking Ending:** Your story can have an unexpected ending. Readers are led to believe that a story will end in a particular way, and then it ends in a different way.

*"The village rejoiced as the evil that had been plaguing them for so long had ended. The sky was blue again and birds were chirping. Peter, happily walking in the field, failed to see the rotting flesh that broke through the soil, snatching him and dragging him under.*

4. **Unhappy or Sad Ending:** Can be more interesting than happy ones and full of emotive impact –so long as it is not overdone. The story can end tragically with the death of the protagonist.

   *In "Romeo and Juliet", Shakespeare sets journey to a very heart-breaking end of a tragic love story.*

5. **Circular ending:** The story circles back to the beginning. It will end with the same idea or similar or exact words at the beginning of the story. Examples include stories where the protagonist returns home after an adventure.

   *In the book 'Alice in wonderland', Alice wakes to find herself again at home.*

   *In 'Wizard of Oz', Dorothy realises "there is no place like home" and she returns back to Kansas.*

   *In 'Lord of the Rings' the hobbits return home after their travels to very exotic lands.*

*end of story*

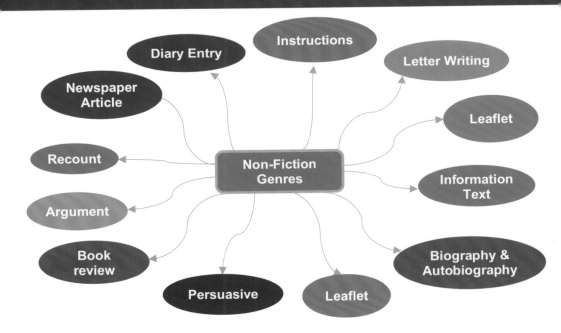

# Balanced Argument

128

**Definition**

- A balanced argument provides information on different points of view and does not lean towards one particular opinion. It allows the readers to make up their own mind.
- When writing a balanced argument, you need to think of 'reasons for' and 'reasons against' your topic. You can do research to get this information.
- You must weigh up your evidence and conclude your argument.

**Examples**

- Should we have uniform at school?
- Should we hunt whales?
- Should capital punishment be made legal?
- Is it ethical to create designer babies?

**Checklist**

- Write an interesting title. One of the ways is to turn the title into a question as it gets the reader thinking. **Example** Are zoos ethical?

- Research to get information about the topic.

- Write an opening paragraph describing the issue that you are going to discuss. **Example** Most people are now questioning the morality of zoos and asking whether they are justified.

- A paragraph for the argument, supported by evidences and examples. **Example** A study suggests that living behind bars can affect the character of the animals by imprisoning them. It gives them little chance to follow their instincts and live naturally.

- A paragraph against the argument, supported by evidences and examples. **Example** However, a zoo with ethics that takes scientific research on animals' behaviour into account, can offer a safe environment for the animals with regular food and protected habitat.

- End with a concluding paragraph to sum it up.

- Keep it balanced and don't use "I think". Try to see the arguments from both sides and ensure that you have been fair to both sides.

**Language Features**

- Write in the present tense unless writing about a historical event.

- Use conjunctions to link points e.g. therefore, in addition to this.

- Use conjunctions to move on to opposing arguments, such as however, although, in comparison to, alternatively.

- Write from the third-person point of view or in an impersonal voice. It makes your writing objective and unbiased.

- Use technical vocabulary to state facts and quotations as an evidence to support your point.

**Definition**

- Persuasive writing is a type of opinion writing. Your opinion is what you think, feel or believe about something. We use persuasive writing to convince someone that our point of view on a subject is right or their point of view is wrong.

- An advertisement, a poster, flier, leaflet, a newspaper article, speech are types of persuasive writing addressing a wider audience and trying to convince them about a product, service or a public issue.

**Examples**

- A flier urging people to vote for or against Brexit.

- A leaflet convincing its audience to buy organic.

- A letter persuading your Head Teacher to take you all to a science museum.

- A leaflet encouraging its audience to recycle.

# Persuasive Writing

## Language

- Think about *PAF (Purpose Audience Form)*.
- Write in the *present tense*. For instance, '*Currently, the break time at schools is not enough.*'
- Use *emotive language and exaggeration*. Overstate the effectiveness or importance of a product or severity of a situation. For example, '*Most of the children are feeling exhausted and finding it extremely hard to focus.*'
- Be *assertive and call for action*. For example, '*Things must change to improve the learning experience of children.*'
- Use *connective phrases* to organise your points. For example, '*In addition, this shows, however*'.
- Use *convincing language and evidence*. For example, use test results, statistics and scientific-sounding jargon. To illustrate, '*Studies suggest that happier children make brighter students, Critics claim that child well-being is of utmost importance, Popular wisdom has it that higher breaktimes increases productivity.*'
- Use *rhetorical questions*. For example, '*Do you want higher results for your schools? Wouldn't happier children make sharper students? Does longer time on task equate to better results or only a greater burnout?*'

## Structure

- **Title:** Eye catching title. It could be a strong statement, a warning or a question. For example, '*Longer Breaktime, Stronger Child Development*' or '*Why is it that so many kids cannot sit still in school today?*'
- Begin with a *question* or a clear presentation of *point of view*.
- Think about what your opponents might argue and include a *counter argument*; either in each paragraph or at the end.
- **Conclusion:** Write an ending that re-states your point of view.
- Use **PEEL structure: Point Evidence Explanation Link** *(Refer card 177)*

**Write an article to raise public awareness of the danger of junk food.**

| Steps | Example |
|---|---|
| Start with an *eye-catching title*. It could be a strong statement, a warning or a question. | • Beware of junk food<br>• Your health, your choice |
| Begin your introduction with a *fact*, a *question* or a quotation, or a *statistic* <br><br>  | • Fast food consumption has risen 500 percent since 1970 and today reaches nearly every part of society, including some public-school cafeterias.<br>• How many times have you eaten fast food this month?<br>• Michelle Obama states, "The problem is when that fun stuff becomes the habit. And I think that's what's happened in our culture. Fast food has become the everyday meal."<br>• Thirty percent of the children in the survey ate fast food on any given day during the survey, and they ate an average of 187 calories a day more than those who did not eat fast food. These additional calories could account for an extra six pounds of weight gain per year, according to Ludwig. |

| Steps | Example |
|---|---|
| Main body that includes at least 3 paragraphs, each starting with an *argument* that would be developed in details through example and | • Argument 1: Increases weight.<br>• Argument 2: Causes high blood pressure.<br>• Argument 3: Leads to sluggishness. |
| Think about what your opponents might argue and include a *counter argument*; either in each paragraph or at the end. | • A fast food company wouldn't agree with the points in this article. They may claim, "It is convenient and harmless in moderation." These arguments just don't hold up when you take all the health impacts into consideration. |
| Write an ending that *re-states your point of view* and you can either *call to action,* provide a *solution*, make a prediction or end with an *open question*. | • "I challenge you to watch what you eat and to avoid fast food."<br>• "Fast food doesn't have to be 'bad food'. Make better choices like salads, fruit and low-fat treats."<br>• "If people continue to eat lots of fast food, they put their health at risk. If kids don't make better choices today, they won't grow into healthy adults."<br>• Are you willing to risk your health? |

**Write a letter to your Head Teacher convincing her to give you a longer breaktime at school.**

| Steps | Example |
|---|---|
| Start with an *eye-catching title*. It could be a strong statement, a warning or a question. | • Do you want happier and smarter students?<br>• The ultimate solution for smarter students. |
| Begin your introduction with a fact, a *question* or a *quotation*, or a *statistic.* | • A 2017 study showed that students with more than 20 minutes of breaktime achieved better grades than those who had less.<br>• Why shouldn't students have a longer breaktime? |
| Main body that includes at least 3 paragraphs, each starting with an *argument* that would be developed in details through examples and explanation. | • Argument 1: Studies show that students tend to be less restless and more attentive in the classroom after breaktime. This also reduces the risk of falling asleep during class. Breaktime allows students to release excess energy they may possess so that their focus can be on schoolwork when they return to the classroom.<br>• Argument 2: Breaktimes also give students the opportunity to process information before returning to class.<br>• Argument 3: Research has shown that 60 minutes of physical activity a day can cumulatively play a valuable role in the prevention and treatment of childhood obesity. |

# Persuasive Writing Example

| Steps | Example |
|---|---|
| Think about what your opponents might argue and include a *counter argument*, either in each paragraph or at the end | • Many people believe that breaktime may be detrimental to learning and to classroom behaviours; however, studies on this topic have proven the opposite. According to a 2009 study, children who received daily breaks were reported to behave better within the classroom |
| Write an ending that *re-states your point of view*. You can either call to *action*, provide a *solution*, make a prediction or end with an open *question*. | • Increasing break time would not only make children happier but will also make them more focused and ultimately improve their grades. |

# Balanced Argument Vs. Persuasive Writing

| | **Balanced Argument** | **Persuasive Writing** |
|---|---|---|
| **Purpose** | • To inform an audience that your viewpoint is worth a consideration. | • To convince an audience to adopt your viewpoint or take a particular action. |
| **Strategy** | • Present information on both sides of a topic. Lay down the merits and demerits by stating claims and counterclaims. | • Emphasise on one side of the argument you are passionate about and call to action. |
| **Phrases** | • While it is true that…. <br> • Opponents will claim… <br> • In spite of the fact… | • You can help… <br> • Do you want…. <br> • We deserve better…. |
| **Style** | • Logical and professional | • Passionate and personal |

**Definition**

- Leaflets are pamphlets or handouts that are circulated to give the reader message/information about something in a small amount of space (one or two sides of a page).

- Leaflets are often distributed free and try to persuade the reader to do something. They are also a cheap and an effective way to advertise.

- Leaflets come in all shapes and sizes, but they all have to tell the reader as much as possible in a small space. They are filled with facts.

**Examples**

- Parks, museums, galleries, local councils, schools and places of historical importance print leaflets to tell people what's on.

- Advertising leaflets printed by shops, hotels and restaurants giving information on things they sell.

- Persuasive leaflets designed by charities to give you information about a campaign to get your support for a particular cause and donate for it.

- Persuasive leaflets by local council encouraging you to recycle or by government urging you to vote for or against something, for example Brexit.

**Structure**

- **Page title** should be clear and bold to grab the readers' attention and make them want to read more.

- **Headings and sub-headings** using different sizes and fonts to structure the information and catch the reader's attention.

- **Main introductory paragraph** giving insight to the reader on what to expect in the leaflet.

- **Diagrams, pictures or photographs with captions and text boxes** are effective tools to convey a lot of information in a small space.

- **Bullet points** to organise the data better.

- **Bright colourful images** to make the leaflet more appealing.

- **Useful information,** such as prices, how to get there, important dates, address, phone number, website address, email address, maps.

- **Persuasive slogans or language, exaggerated language, rhetorical questions** to engage and persuade the audience.

- **Call to action with a clear message** urging the readers to vote a certain way or donate for a certain cause, call a particular number or log on to a website. **Example** Buy Now! Call for more details, Donate using the below link.

# Blurb

**Definition**

- A blurb is a short description of the book printed on its back cover.
- It is written by the author or the publisher to promote the book. It could also be a quotation from the reader praising the book.
- It should be written in a way so that whoever reads the blurb must want to read it more.
- The trick is to give away enough of what is inside the book. Do not give any plot spoilers for fiction or too many details for non-fiction.

**Structure**

- If your book has a strong theme or genre then bring it out. Is it about bonds of friendship, or betrayal? Is it 'a deeply moving story of family and friendship'?
- Create interest around the main conflict.
- Dive right in and introduce your main character.
- Keep it short and punchy. You need to draw the reader in quickly and hold their attention.
- Use key words like 'secret', 'mystery', 'betrayal', 'revenge', 'magic' to whet the reader's appetite.

Below are few examples of blurbs of the same book. Notice how the use of different techniques (rhetorical questions, figures of speech, exciting adjectives) create interesting blurbs.

- Who or what is Endymion Spring? A voiceless boy with a terrible secret? A book that feeds on children? A door to boundless power and forbidden knowledge?

- A cloaked figure drags a heavy box through the snow-covered streets in the darkest night. The chest, covered in images of mythical beasts, can only be opened when the fangs of its serpent's head taste blood.

- Centuries later, in an Oxford library, a boy touches a strange book and feels something pierce his finger. A timeless secret is unfolding. And the mystery has only just begun.

- A completely absorbing tale of hidden myths and dangerous knowledge, which tightly grips you from the very first page, and refuses to let go. Every page reveals new secrets every second and your eyes cannot possibly stray elsewhere.

- "Quite simply the best book I've read. Endymion Spring is fantastically frightening, absorbingly exciting and all round excellent. And one question torments you throughout: What is Endymion Spring? All answers lie within. Enter at your own peril!"

**Definition**

- A book review is a thorough description, critical analysis and evaluation of the content, style and merit of the book.

- Give your honest (positive or negative) and detailed thoughts in a review which people can use to find new books that are right for them.

**Structure**

- The book's title and author
- Begin with an opinion or a question
- A brief summary of the plot that doesn't give away too much
- Comments on the book's strengths and weaknesses
- Conclude with the reviewer's personal response to the book with specific examples to support praise or criticism
- Write in present tense.

Checklist

- Does the review briefly sum up the main parts of the book?
- Does the book fit into a genre, such as mystery or romance, and why?
- When and where does the action in the book take place? Does the author do a good job of making you feel like you are there? How?
- Does your review talk about how the book interested you? Did the book make you laugh or cry or left you guessing?
- Does your review adequately describe characters of the story? Are the main characters believable? Do you know anyone like them?
- What do you like or dislike about the author's writing style? – the ending or characters or anything else in the story.
- Use concrete examples to back up your points, such as describing a scene that really moved you. You can also use a couple of short quotations from the book.
- Round up your review by summarizing your thoughts. Would you recommend the book? Who would you recommend it to (young or old)? Are there any books or series you would compare it to?
- What star rating would you give it?

### Tuck Everlasting *by Natalie Babbitt*

This book is about a special spring that gives eternal life to those who drink from it. Ten-year-old Winnie Foster stumbles on the secret of the Tuck family while exploring the woods. The family kidnaps her to keep their secret intact. There she meets Jesse Tuck and gets drawn to the unusual life of his family. The family explains to her that living forever at one age is less of a blessing than it might seem.

This refreshing book describes various moral dilemmas and invites the reader to reflect on everlasting life and its advantages and disadvantages. Is it a boon or a burden? It examines the weighty idea of "forever" with a touch of simplicity.

The book is set in beautiful surroundings with breath-taking descriptions of the landscape. The vivid description of the characters adds to the merit of the book.

The book will make a compelling read for both young and old.

This book is intense, powerful, exciting and poignant. I would definitely recommend reading it and give it a 5-star rating.

**Definition**

- An information text is a piece of non-fiction writing which informs the readers about a particular thing or a subject.

- Examples include technical texts, Science or History books, instruction manuals.

**Features**

- Use of *technical vocabulary* and *formal language*.

- Title informing what the text is about.

- Use of features like **bold,** underlined and coloured texts so the important information stands out.

- Sub-headings to organize the piece of writing into sections.

- Bullet points to organise the data.

- Use of pictures with captions or labelled diagrams.

- Use of tables, graphs and charts where needed.

## Sharks [Bold Title] [Technical Vocabulary]

Sharks are a group of around 400 marine fish. All have the torpedo-shaped bodies, skeletons made of cartilage, exposed gill slits, powerful tails, teeth that are replaced throughout their lives and airplane wing-like pectoral fins.

### Life Span [Sub-headings]

The life spans range from 20 to 30 years for most of the species. The dogfish and whale shark can live up to 100 years. Scientists can tell the age of a shark by counting the rings on its vertebrae (similar to how they can tell how old a tree is by counting its rings!)

### What makes them a good predator

Sharks have good underwater vision and acute senses for hunting their prey. They can detect tiny amounts of chemicals in the water – as little as one drop of blood. They have lateral line pores for sensing sound and motion. They can pick up electrical signals as tiny as those created by the muscles of their prey.

### Always on the move

Sharks are almost always on the move. For one thing, they are hungry. But many must swim to avoid sinking because they lack an air bladder, which helps other fish stay afloat when not moving. Others cannot pump water over their gills, so they cannot breathe unless they swim.

### Did you know?

- Most of today's sharks developed 64 million years ago – when the dinosaurs were around!

- Shark skin is tough and hard. Before the invention of sandpaper it was used to polish wood.

- Stragely the largest sharks tend to be the most harmless, they eat plankton by swimming with their jaws wide open.

**Write an information text about how the water cycle works.**

<u>Checklist</u>

- Start with a relevant and a clear title.

- A short opening paragraph about clouds and rain and how water is constantly recycling itself.

- Include sub-headings to define all the technical vocabulary such as, evaporation, condensation, precipitation, percolation, transpiration.

- Explain the above process or stages in a chronological order.

- Include relevant diagrams with captions.

- Include a concluding paragraph. Can include fun facts such as, more than 75% of Earth's surface is covered in water.

- Use the text features like **Bold**, Coloured Text and <u>Underlines</u>.

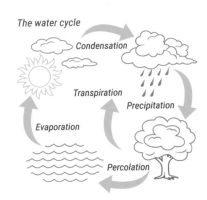

**Definition**

- Instructions are a step-by-step guide that tells us how to do or make something.

- They are written for someone who needs to know how to do or make something.

- Examples include *"Instructions on how to cook a recipe", "Build a model", "Play a game", "Gardening Guide", or "Get from one place to another".*

**Structure**

- Write an appropriate title with the end goal.

- Write a list of equipment and ingredients.

- Write steps in order using numbers, letters or bullet points.

- Write in the present tense.

- Using *imperative verbs* or bossy verbs, or occasionally adverbs (Gently, Carefully, Swiftly), to begin each step

- Write in second person.

- Use easy to understand language appropriate for the audience.

## How to bake a Cake

### Ingredients

120 grams softened butter, 1 cup of sugar, 2 medium eggs, 2.5 spoons of baking powder, 1.5 cups of flour

### Instructions

1. Make sure the ingredients are at a room temperature.

2. Preheat oven to 180C/fan 160C.

3. Grease and line a baking tin with baking parchment and keep it aside.

4. Mix butter and sugar together in a large bowl until pale and fluffy.

5. Then beat in the eggs to this mixture until the mixture is thick and voluminous.

6. Gently fold in the flour using large metal spoon, working in a gentle figure of 8 motion to preserve all the air you've whisked in. Keep going until no dry lumps of flour remain.

7. Pour the mixture in the greased tin.

8. Bake for 25-30 minutes. The sponge should rise, appear golden and feel springy to the touch.

9. Leave to cool in the tin for 5-10 minutes, then release by running a knife around the edge.

**Definition**

- Letters are messages and are used for different reasons: to tell someone something, to complain, to ask for information, or to apply for something, such as a job.

- Letters are organised under two headings: Formal Letters and Informal Letters.

- Formal letters are sent to people you do not know personally. They can be sent for different reasons; for example, to complain about something, to give or ask for information or to make an appointment or a job application.

**Structure**

- **Header:** Your (or sender's) Address and Date

- **Recipient's Name and Address:** Write their title and full name when you know it. Or write a designation such as, *The Principal, Customer Support, HR Manager* when you do not know the name.

- **Salutation or Greeting:** *'Dear Sir or Madam'*, when you do not know the name of the person you are writing to. *'Dear Mr./Mrs./Dr. Last Name'*, when you know the name of the person you are writing to.

- **Main Body**
  - An introduction, stating the purpose of letter and who you are.
  - Reason for your writing – complaint, request or information, job application.
  - A conclusion, including any expectations or closing remarks. Do not end the letter abruptly.

- **Closing Farewell and Signature:** *'Yours Faithfully'*, when you do not know the name of the person you are writing to. *'Yours Sincerely'*, when you know the name of the person you are writing to. Sign off your name and/or signature.

*Write a letter to your headteacher complaining about the quality of food served in the cafeteria.*

**Your Name and Address**

Ms Eva Markle
64 North Street
RM2 345

**Date** — 20th Nov 2018

Mr. Hart
Bright School
12 The Drive
RM1 775

**Recipient's Name and Address**

Dear Mr. Hart,

**Salutation or Greeting**

**Introduction**

**Reason of your writing**

**Main Body**

My name is Eva Markle and I am a year five student. I am writing to inform you about the poor quality of the food in the cafeteria. Several of my classmates have also noticed this situation and agree with my complaint.

The food is not covered and attracts a lot of flies. This is very unhygienic and we are very worried as two of my friends have fallen sick after eating the cafeteria food. We would also like to highlight that the rubbish bin in the cafeteria are not emptied every day. This causes bad smell and poor sanitation conditions.

We believe these complaints are fair and can be fixed if you will act to solve these matters.

Thank you for your time.

Yours Sincerely,
Eva Markle

**Closing Farewell and Your name**

**Conclusion**

**Definition**

- **Informal letters** are letters which are sent to people you know. For example, sending a postcard telling someone about your holiday, to say, "thank you" for a birthday present or writing to friends or family who might live a long way from you.

**Structure**

- **Header:** Your (or sender's) Address and Date

- **Salutation or Greeting**: *'Dear (First Name)'*

- **Main Body:**

  o   Use friendly informal language.

  o   Ask the recipient questions that will encourage a response.

  o   Use connectives effectively.

  o   In the concluding paragraph, ask the recipient to respond (e.g. keep in touch). Do not end the letter abruptly.

- **Closing Farewell and Your Name/Nickname:** *'Yours sincerely'*, *'Yours'*, or even *'Love From'* if you know them really well.

*Write a letter to your friend*

Your Address

64 North Street
RM2 345

Date

20th Nov 2018

Salutation or Greeting

Dear Katie,

Main Body

Thank you for your letter. It was so good to hear from you and read all about your Paris holiday.

All is well with us. I am preparing for my SATs and Eleven Plus Exams, which sure keeps me super busy. My swimming practice is going well, I came first in the last swimming gala and won a trophy!

I can't wait for my exams to be over so I can come and visit you. We have to go to that ice-cream parlour again and enjoy the "all you can eat" deal. I still have a smile on my face whenever I think about how much we ate the last time we went there.

I must end the letter now as I have to rush to my swimming lessons. Love to your sister and do write to me soon.

Love,
Anna

Closing Farewell and Your name

Conclusion

|  | Formal | Informal |
|---|---|---|
| **Salutation** | • Dear Mr/Mrs + Surname<br>• Dear Sir or Madam | • Hello / Hi + Name<br>• Dear + Name<br>• Hi there! |
| **Introduction** | • Thank you for your letter/email about…<br>• Many thanks for your letter/email.<br>• I am writing to request information about / inform you about / complain about, apologise for…<br>• I am writing with reference to your letter.<br>• I would like to offer congratulations on…<br>• Let me congratulate you on… | • Thanks for your letter/email.<br>• Thanks for writing to me.<br>• It was great to hear from you again.<br>• I am writing to tell you about…<br>• Guess what?<br>• How are things with you? / What's up? / How are you? / How was your holiday?<br>• I'm sorry I haven't written for a while. |

|  | Formal | Informal |
|---|---|---|
| **Conclusion** | • I look forward to hearing from you without delay.<br><br>• I look forward to meeting you.<br><br>• I hope to hear from you at your earliest convenience | • Hope to hear from you soon.<br><br>• Looking forward to seeing you / hearing from you.<br><br>• I can't wait to meet up soon.<br><br>• Write back soon. |
| **Closing Farewell** | • If you start with 'Dear Sir or Madam', finish with 'Yours faithfully',<br><br>• If you start with 'Dear Mr/Mrs…', finish with 'Yours sincerely'.<br><br>• Regards / Best Regards / Kind Regards | • Best Wishes<br><br>• Love<br><br>• All the best<br><br>• Keep in touch |

**Definition**

- A recount retells an event or an experience that has happened in the past. It is written to inform or entertain the reader or to assess the events.

- Examples include diaries, newspaper and magazines articles, autobiographies, biographies, experiences such as a school picnic, visit to a football match, talent show at school, reports on historical events like a famous battle or development of an invention.

- Newspaper reports and reports on historical events are factual recounts where the writer may not necessarily be involved in the events.

**Features**

- Title informing the reader what are you writing about.

- Introductory paragraph briefly covering Who, What, When, Where and Why.

- Paragraphs in chronological order, to follow the order of events, similar to a timeline.

- Write only about the interesting parts; you don't want to bore your audience.

- It is written in the past tense as it describes an event or an experience that has already happened.

- It is written in the first or the third person.

- Use of connectives such as first, then, next, after that, eventually, finally.

- Personal comments and quotations can be included.

- Concluding paragraph summarising the main points.

**Definition**

- 'Bio' meaning 'life' and 'graphy' meaning 'I write'.

- Biography is a true story of person's life that is written by someone else. The characters, setting and events are real. For example, *"Bill Gates: A Biography"*

- Biographies are written for people who have made a significant contribution to the society in any field.

- The writer must carry out lots of research of the person they are writing about to give an accurate account of the subject. The research may include meeting the person who is being written about. It helps the reader understand why the person is successful, interesting or famous.

**Structure**

- Biographies are written in the third person. The narrator uses the pronouns such as he, she, her, his, him to refer to the subject. For example: *"After dropping out of Harvard, Bill Gates and his partner Paul Allen set about revolutionizing the computer industry."*

- Throughout the biography you witness the subject's (main character's) struggles and successes in life.

- Most biographies are written in a chronological order (arranged in the order of time).

**Definition**

- A timeline provides a visual representation of events that helps you better understand history, a story, or a process.

- Creating a timeline of the individual's important life events can help you write the biography.

---

**Example: Timeline of Steve Jobs**

- February 1955: Steve Paul Jobs is born in California and adopted by Paul and Clara Jobs.

- 1971 to 1975: Steve Jobs meets Wozniak at high school, drops out of college and builds the world's first Apple I in his bedroom.

- April 1976: 'Apple Computers' is founded in Job's family garage.

- December 1980: Apple goes Public.

- 1985: Apple forces Steve Jobs to resign. He picks himself up very quickly and starts working on his new computer building company called 'Next'.

- 1997: Steve Jobs becomes interim CEO and chairman of Apple Computer Inc.

- 1998: Steve Jobs unveils Apple's revolutionary iMac.

- 2000: Steve Jobs becomes permanent CEO of Apple.

- 2006: MacBook Pro and Apple TV are released.

- 2007: The first iPhone is released, one of the first phones without keyboard.

- 2011: Apple releases iPad 2, iCloud and iPhone 4s. Steve Jobs delivers his last ever keynote.

- 2011: October 2011 Steve Jobs dies of pancreatic cancer.

- Write a biography for your favourite sports person. You can use internet and non-fiction books to find information on their early life, education, major accomplishments, interesting facts as events shaping the person's life, obstacles they overcame and family life.

- Use an interesting opening statement or question to hook the reader.
- Summarise the main events of the person's life in the first few paragraphs.
- Write in the past tense.
- Use third person pronouns; examples include he, she, his, her, they, them, their.
- Write about the key events and key influences in the subject's in life.
- Before you begin writing, create a timeline to list the series of events in the person's life in a chronological order.

**Definition**

- 'Auto' means self, bio' meaning 'life' and 'graphy' meaning 'I write'.

- It is a **self-written** account of someone's life. The subject may write about what has influenced them and include details of their feelings during different experiences they have had. For example, *"My life and work – An autobiography of Henry Ford."*

- Throughout the autobiography the reader learns about key incidents or events of the individual's life.

**Structure**

- Autobiography is written in the first person. The narrator uses the pronouns such as I, me, my, mine, we, our, ours, we and us. Example, '*In Henry Ford's autobiography, he writes, "I am not a reformer. I think there is entirely too much attempt at reforming in the world and that we pay too much attention to reformers."*

- Most autobiographies are written in a chronological order (arranged in the order of time).

Both biography and autobiography are **non-fictional** and **factual**. Characters in both are family and friends of the person. The setting (time and place) for both will be where the person lived, when the person lived. Both are written in **chronological order** (mostly). They are written by or for people who have made a significant contribution to the society in any field.

| Biography | Autobiography |
|---|---|
| Written by someone other than the subject | Written by the person it is about or a ghost writer |
| Written in the third person | Written in the first person |
| The perspective is factual | The perspective is facts, thoughts and feelings |
| The author's purpose is to inform | The author's purpose is to express |
| Example, 'Hard Drive: Bill Gates, and 'The Making of Microsoft Empire' by James Wallace and Jim Erickson | Example, 'Humble Pie' by Gordon Ramsay |

**Are the following statements more likely to be found in Biographies or Autobiographies?**

1. He was born and grew up in London, moving to France at the age of 13.

2. I never enjoyed writing until I met my idol, Jacqueline Wilson, who ignited my interest.

3. Dancing became my passion. I would dance every day and used to get angry and frustrated when I was told off for practising in the living room. I think my mother was always more concerned about me knocking over her priceless ornaments.

4. He was born in Wales on 13th September 1916. His father died when he was 3 years old and his mother brought him up. He died at the age of 98, with his family at his bedside.

5. I am crying. I am a Sheffield schoolgirl writing in her diary about the bullies awaiting me tomorrow.

6. Our little room perhaps looked bare at first with nothing on the walls; but thanks to Daddy who had brought my film star collection and postcards beforehand and with aid of paste, pot and brush, I have transformed the walls into one gigantic picture.

7. "She never could sit still at school!" was the comment made by Mrs Alice Hall, an old teacher of hers.

1. Biography

2. Autobiography

3. Autobiography

4. Biography

5. Autobiography.

6. Autobiography.

7. Biography

# Diary Writing

**Definition**

- A diary entry is a section of writing that has been organized by date. The periodic entries are expressions of your thoughts, feelings and opinions. These entries break up your diary into smaller pieces like chapters of a book.

**Features**

- Write in the first person.
- Write an introduction to set the scene.
- Write in the past tense.
- Describe the important events.
- Describe the place where the event happened.
- Use time connectors such as, *first, then, lastly, in the end, before, next, after* to show when the things happened.
- Write about feelings, opinions and reactions.
- Use personal pronouns such as, *I, we, my, me* from writer's point of view.
- Use paragraphs to organise events.

Writing a diary is often an expression of writer's feelings, opinions and reactions to events. Since there can be more than one way to perceive an event, 'diary accounts' of the same event can be very different.

Look at the following two diary entries of the same event, a brother and a sister attending a football match. See how both the accounts are different.

Following techniques have been used in both the pieces:

- **Simile**

- **Metaphor**

- **Hyperbole**

- **Personification**

- **Onomatopoeia**

- **Oxymoron**

Observe how the use of these techniques has made the piece of writing interesting and vivid.

20th September 2019

The drive was long and my eyes started to crack as miles of roads piled up before me. Finally, as my muscles surrendered and my heavy eyelids were tired of sight, I hugged the blackness as my senses diminished.

After an hour of blackness, cheers woke me up and I realised we had reached the stadium.

Adrenaline burst through me like a rocket of immense power. I jumped up into the sunroof ignoring the warnings of my parents. We were here. My heart was in my mouth as I grabbed my bag and raced to my seat. Time froze as I witnessed Rooney swing his leg against the ball, smashing it to his teammate before the two cornered the defence and scored. A goal in the first minute! I added that to the list of things that proved my team was the best.

The tension and excitement in the air mixed with smell of chips and sauce gave the stadium a unique but weird atmosphere with different people feeling very differently. I glanced back to my sister as she glared at her phone screen. I tried to ignore the fact that she has just disrespected something very close to my heart. I oriented myself back to the pitch where the teams were hovering around the goals but no one was scoring. As an act of desperation, my team had started kicking balls everywhere but none went in the goal.

As my team chased towards the goal, I jumped up in the air and whistled as if trying to blow the ball further into the goal. It was happening. The crowd boomed in my ears as the closest defender missed the ball and also tripped on the goalkeeper, banging him in the head. My sister was clearly confused as she stared down at the stadium. The score was settled 2:1, and with 90 seconds left I couldn't be more joyful as it was an awfully good match full of excitement.

20<sup>th</sup> September 2019

There was not much to write about today but I decided to put pen on paper just for the sake of it. I can tell you now you will pity me.

For starters, I got a million miles of long road that my brother could endure, but I had no reason to. My phone had run out of battery and I felt like a bird in a cage with nothing to do. After hours of boredom, I surrendered and entered the peaceful world that my brother and mother were already in. I was thankful as the boredom was washed away with dreams.

I was rudely awoken by the noise of my parents shouting at my brother- typical. He sprinted into the stadium like a rabbit without waiting for the people that had brought him here in the first place.

He sat with his eyes glued to the pitch. Suddenly he started to dance around like a monkey. I stared at the pitch and realised that one of the 'men', or moving dots on the ground, had put the ball in the goal using his leg.

The atmosphere was electric. I glanced at my brother and he was nibbling his nails like a hamster. I tried to act naturally as if I knew what was happening but it probably showed that I was clearly confused.

The match was dull and boring although alongside it there was a much better match going on: manager wars. They were like two repelling magnets and were hard to ignore. There couldn't be anything more hilarious. It was the only thing that kept me from dozing off.

## Simile

- *'adrenaline burst through me like a rocket of immense power'*
- *'like monkeys jumping in the air'*
- *'like a bird in a cage'*
- *'like two repelling magnets'*
- *'sprinted like a rabbit'*
- *'dance around like a monkey'*

## Oxymoron

- *'clearly confused'*
- *'awfully good'*
- *'act naturally'*

## Alliteration

- *'million miles'*

## Hyperbole

- *'my team was the best'*
- *'there couldn't be anything more hilarious'*
- *'million miles'*

## Personification

- *'time froze'*
- *'muscles surrendered'*
- *'hugged blackness'*

## Onomatopoeia

- *'banging'*

## Metaphor

- *'eyes glued to the pitch'*

**Definition**

- News reports inform the reader of what is happening in the world. They follow a certain structure and answer the following six questions.

**Six Questions**

- **WHO** is involved? Who does it affect? Who witnessed the event?

- **WHAT** happened in the story?

- **WHEN** did the event take place?

- **WHERE** did the story take place? Was more than one location involved?

- **WHY** did the event take place? Why is it important to tell this story?

- **HOW** did it happen?

Newspaper reports follow an 'Inverted Pyramid' format. It has the most important information about a story in the lead paragraph. This ensures that if the story needs to be cut short by the editor, he can still cut the last paragraphs, and your story will still make sense and feel complete. This is what it looks like:

**Most important information (6 Ws)**
*Who? What? Where? When? How?*

**Less important infomation**

*Quotaions, Expert Opinions, Statistics*

Similar or
related
events

1. **Headline** Large and bold so it stands out. The headline must be punchy to grab the reader's attention. Use features such as alliteration, pun, rhyme, rhetoric question to make it catchy. Converting the headline into a question can intrigue the reader.

2. **Introduction/Lead Paragraph** This section briefly summaries the events. Make it interesting so the reader is hooked and wants to continue to read. It must contain all the key information and leave the less important information for the subsequent paragraphs. Sometimes it is the only part of the story that people read. Briefly cover **Who/ What/ When/ Where/ Why/ How** in the opening paragraph.

3. **Body** It gives more details and provides more information on the six W's of the story. Continue to write in the order of importance, giving the most important information first, categorise the text into paragraphs.

4. **Images (with captions)/Statistics/Tables/Diagrams** These features pique the readers' interest and helps them to understand and visualise the story better.

5. **Quotations and Interviews** Give the viewpoint of someone involved in the story (witnesses and experts) to make the report more interesting and credible. Use correct punctuation for quotations.

6. **Conclusion** Sums up and brings the story up-to-date on what is happening next. Includes concluding statements and/or opinions from witnesses.

**Language Features**

- Use formal language and actual details rather than thoughts and feelings.

- Write in the third person using pronouns such as, he, she, they, them and it.

- Write in the past tense (newspaper reports are mostly recounts).

- Keep the sentences short and punchy.

- A use of rhetorical questions encourages the reader to agree with you.

- Newspaper report must be easy to understand.

- Be fair and include both sides of the story; don't let your personal opinion come in between reporting facts.

- Write in a chronological order.

- Include facts and quotations from eyewitnesses.

- The concluding paragraph can include opinions of the eyewitnesses and what will happen next.

## White Taj Mahal turning Green and Brown with Pollution

Thanks to pollution, bug excrement, and particulates thrown into the air by construction in the vicinity, the Taj Mahal its changing colour. Constructed primarily using white marble in the 17th century, the UNESCO world heritage site has changed in colour from white to a troublesome yellow and, more recently, has become sullied with shades of brown and green.

According to the BBC, the Indian Supreme Court recently criticized the country's government for allowing the site to fall into such disrepair, with one court justice saying, "Even if you have the expertise, you are not utilizing it. Or perhaps you don't care."

For its part, the Indian government has moved to protect the Taj Mahal in the past: it forced the closure of thousands of factories near the site in an effort to protect the building and grounds from pollution. Unfortunately, fighting pollution in the area is an uphill battle. The mausoleum, located in the city of Agra, sits adjacent to the Yamuna River. The river is rife with raw sewage, which attracts hordes of insects, which apparently love to poop on the world heritage site. On several occasions over the past couple of decades, the Indian government has attempted to clean the exterior of the building, in the hopes of bringing it back to its original colouring. However, their efforts have had little to no effect.

Given the Taj Mahal's importance as a tourist destination (it draws close to 70,000 people per day) and its cultural significance, India's Supreme Court has ordered the country's government to seek foreign help to bring the building back to its former glory. It has ordered the Indian government to form a committee to implement corrective measures by September 15th 2020 at the very latest.

### 3 Sure ways to ruin your SATs
Start your preparation last minute; you work the best under pressure. Sleep is overrated; study all night to get more done. Use only practice papers, no need to get a grip on the text books, it's just too much work.

### Hurricane Michael leaves death, devastation & diseases behind
The death toll from Hurricane Michael rose to 20 after 5 more bodies were found on Friday. The search and rescue teams confirmed that the numbers are likely to increase as they continue to evacuate the disaster areas.
The hurricane wreaked havoc leaving behind flooded buildings and shattered lives.

### Is it possible to stop identity theft?
Methods of identity theft are evolving rapidly. With the explosion of social media, people's identities are more exposed than ever. Identity theft appears impossible to eradicate; however, its likelihood can be reduced by taking certain precautions and being careful about our privacy settings.

### 3D printed arms give new life to the amputees
The bionic 3D printed arm launched by Robotic Bionics has developed the first medically certified 3D arm. The arm costs as little as £5500 and can fit anyone over the age of seven. It has brought hope for many.

**Using the 'Inverted Pyramid' structure, write a newspaper article about one of the following topics:**

1. A recent sporting event

2. A scientific discovery

3. A political event

## PEEL (Point Evidence Explanation Link)

**PEEL** is a technique used to write creative essays, argumentative or persuasive pieces of writing. It provides structure and depth for each point you make, helping you create clear and powerful paragraphs.

- State a clear and a relevant **point** about the topic.

- Find **evidence** to support your point. Use quotations or events from the text.

- **Explain** your evidence and how it supports your point. What effect does this evidence have and how does it prove your point?

- **Link** back to the point or to the next point in the following paragraph. What does this point and evidence have to do with the question?

| Point | Evidence | Explanation | Link |
|---|---|---|---|
| • It has been suggested that… | • The source tells us that… | • The source clearly indicates… | • All this evidence demonstrates that… |
| • It is believed that… | • This is demonstrated by… | • This shows us that… | • Therefore, it is evident that… |
| • Some people argue that… | • This is supported by… | • It is clear from this that… | • In conclusion… |
| • One school of thought is… | • This is shown in… | • This demonstrates that… | • This tells you that… |
| • One argument is that… | • For example….. | • It appears that… | • This is why…. |
| • Many people believe that… | • For instance…. | • This supports the argument by… | |
| • To begin with… | • Consider the example of… | • The evidence explains that… | |
| • One reason for… | | • As a result of… | |
| • One point of view.. | | • This means that… | |

| Point | Evidence | Explanation | Link |
|---|---|---|---|
| Some Christians argue that God made plants and animals for us, so we can change them to fit our requirements and needs. | This is supported by a quotation from the Bible, "And let them have dominion over the fish of the sea and over the birds of the heavens and over the livestock and over all the earth and over every creeping thing that creeps on the earth." | The verse shows that we are above all the plants and animals and therefore genetic modification should be allowed as animals and plants were made to live under us so we can do whatever seems fit. | Therefore, it is evident that humans, as a species, have the right to genetically modify and clone plants and animals. |

| Point | Evidence | Explanation | Link |
|---|---|---|---|
| Some people believe that homework is an important tool for learning and in turn achieving higher scores. | In a study conducted by Hill, Spencer, Alston and Fitzgerald (1986), homework was positively linked to student achievement. | This study clearly indicates that homework is an effective method of improving student academic preparation because improved student achievement is linked with greater rates of learning. | So, we can conclude that to improve learning and achieving higher score in any of the school subjects, we have to practice the questions related to the appointed topics and homework provides the necessary practice. |
| On the other hand, I would argue that homework takes up more time and students need that time out of school to relax and do activities such as sports, so homework should not be given. | According to Richard Walker, an educational psychologist at Sydney University, data shows that in countries where more time is spent on homework, students' score lower on a standardized test. | It appears that inundating children with hours of homework each night is detrimental to the child's progress. | In conclusion, I would like to reiterate my earlier statement that all schools must stop giving homework. |

| Point | Evidence | Explanation | Link |
|-------|----------|-------------|------|
| Some people believe that the time has come for drastic measures and cars must be banned from the city to reduce pollution. | In central London the average annual levels of pollution are almost double the WHO limit of 10 µg/m3. | London is widely recognised as the worst area for air pollution in the UK. There is growing evidence that dangerously polluted air is damaging people's health in towns and cities across the country. | In light of the scale of the crisis, more urgent and immediate action is required. A ban on the cars in the centre of the cities would therefore seem sensible, as it would cut pollution thereby improving health. |
| On the other, it could be argued that such a ban would create other problems of public transport. | Research reveals that London has the highest public transport fares in the world, when compared with other global cities. The public transport of the country is expensive and sometimes unreliable. | Therefore, it is evident that banning cars in the city cannot be a viable solution. While there is an urgent need, we must find alternate solutions like using cleaner fuels and encouraging people to use public transport rather than forcing them to do so. | In conclusion the effects and problems caused outweigh the benefit of banning cars completely. So, banning cars is not a viable solution. |

**Are Zoos ethical?**

- This clearly proves that wild animals belong to their natural habitat and not captive prison like environment.

- It is believed that removing wild animals from their natural habitat is extremely cruel.

- A government-funded study in UK zoos found that 54% of the elephants and 48% of Lions showed behavioural problems during the daytime.

- Therefore, we can conclude that we must end the suffering of the animals by freeing them from the zoos.

**Walk to School**

- A 7-year study of 1700 high school students in England predicted that obesity prevalence would decrease by 22 percent if children walked or biked to school four or five days a week.

- This study demonstrates that children who walked or biked to school are more active and less likely to be overweight and obese compared to other children who don't.

- Walking or riding to school is better than driving to school.

- This tells us clearly that we must encourage children to walk or bike to school and discourage dependence on cars.

**Vegetarianism 3**

- This study clearly indicates that vegetarians have a healthier diet, which supports a better immune system that can help prevent and reverse certain chronic diseases.

- One school of thought is that a vegetarian diet is a healthier diet and helps to live longer.

- This tells that the vegetarian diet is better as it enables a longer life span.

- This claim is supported by the British Medical Journal, which states that vegetarians outlive meat eaters by six years as the diet is generally rich in fibre, antioxidants, and minerals, which in turn strengthen the immune system.

**Vegetarianism 4**

- This is why vegetarians are believed to have a lower BMI.

- The Oxford Vegetarian Study found that BMI levels are lower in vegetarians for all age groups and for both men and women.

- The evidence suggests that Vegetarians have a lower BMI due to a fibre-rich diet.

- It is believed that vegetarians have a lower body mass index (BMI) compared to meat eaters, as vegetarian diets tend to be naturally low in saturated fat and cholesterol.

## Point

It is believed that removing wild animals from their natural habitat is extremely cruel.

## Evidence

A government-funded study in UK zoos found that 54% of the elephants and 48% of Lions showed behavioural problems during the daytime.

## Explanation

This study clearly proves that wild animals belong to their natural habitat and not prison-like environment.

## Link

Therefore, we can conclude that we must end the suffering of animals by freeing them from zoos.

Can you think of the other side of the argument?

| Point | Evidence | Explanation | Link |
|-------|----------|-------------|------|
| Walking or riding to school is better than driving to school. | A 7-year study of 1700 high school students in England predicted that obesity prevalence would decrease by 22 percent if children walked or biked to school four or five days a week. | This study demonstrates that children who walked or biked to school are more active and less likely to be overweight and obese compared to other children who don't. | This tells us clearly that we must encourage children to walk or bike to school and discourage dependence on cars. |

Can you think of the other side of the argument?

| Point | Evidence | Explanation | Link |
|---|---|---|---|
| One school of thought is that a vegetarian diet is a healthier diet and helps to live longer. | This claim is supported by the British Medical Journal, which states that vegetarians outlive meat eaters by six years as the diet is generally rich in fibre, antioxidants, and minerals, which in turn strengthen the immune system. | This study clearly indicates that vegetarians have a healthier diet, which supports a better immune system that can help prevent and reverse certain chronic diseases. | This tells that the vegetarian diet is better as it enables a longer life span. |
| It is believed that vegetarians have a lower body mass index (BMI) compared to meat eaters, as vegetarian diets tend to be naturally low in saturated fat and cholesterol. | The Oxford Vegetarian Study found that BMI levels are lower in vegetarians for all age groups and for both men and women. | The evidence suggests that Vegetarians have a lower BMI due to a fibre-rich diet. | This is why vegetarians are believed to have a lower BMI. |

**Definition**

- Parts of speech describe words in a sentence based on their grammatical function.

**Examples**

- **Noun** is name of a person, place, thing, feeling or an idea
- **Pronoun** replaces a noun to avoid repetition
- **Adjective** describes or gives more information about a noun or a pronoun
- **Verb** is an action word or state/situation
- **Adverb** describes a verb, adjective or another adverb. Answers how, where, when.
- **Preposition** shows the relationship of a noun/pronoun to another word(s).
- **Conjunction** joins two words, ideas, phrase together
- **Interjection** is word or phrase that expresses emotion/feelings
- **Article/Determiner** precedes a noun or an adjective describing a noun. (a, an, the)

**Definition**

- Name of a person, place, thing, feeling and idea.

  - *The children were filled with joy as they ate their sandwiches at a picnic with their friends at Hyde park.*

---

**Examples**

- **Common Noun:** Name of the group or class of objects, person, place or thing. *Examples include elephant, boy, mother, toddler, student, playground, pens, cricket.*

- **Collective Noun:** Name for a collection or a number of objects or people. *Examples include a group of boys, a herd of cows, a shoal of fish, a pack of wolves, an army of soldiers.*

- **Abstract Noun:** Name of a quality, feeling or state, things you cannot touch. *Examples include kindness, darkness, love, anger, death, poverty, wisdom, judgement, youth, music.*

- **Proper Noun:** Name of a particular person, place or thing and always begins with a capital letter. *Examples include Jamie, England, Earth, Thames.*

**Definition**

- Pronouns are words that can be used instead of nouns or to replace a noun to avoid repetition. *Examples include I, you, he, she, it, we, me, her, his, him, their, they, them.*

**Examples**

- **Relative pronouns** are used to connect a phrase or clause to a noun or pronoun. *Examples include which, who, whose, where, when, that.*

  - *A mother is someone who always nourishes.*

  - *I have an uncle whose car is amazing.*

  - *I want to go to a store where they sell cheap gadgets.*

  - *A vehicle is something that transports people and goods.*

  - *The electric car, which everyone is talking about, is very expensive.*

- **Possessive pronoun** are used to show ownership. *Examples include mine, yours, his, hers, ours, theirs, its.*

  - *The black bag in the garage is mine and the one on the shelf is yours.*

  - *We shall rightfully have what is ours.*

**Definition**

- Words that are used to add more information about the noun or pronoun. They describe attributes, size, age, temperature, measurement, nationality or origin, material, feeling or qualities etc. Some sentences can have more than one adjective.

- *Examples include large, golden, interesting, twenty, pleasant, Spanish, young, wooden.*

**Examples**

- Sonia is a lovey Indian girl with a beautiful smile.
- She received a silver pendant as a present.
- He had a miserable childhood.
- On her birthday she received a red sports car.
- They live in a cosy wooden cottage.

**Definition**

- Words that can are used to express actions like run, sit, sleep, eat or a state of being such as to enjoy, to have, to like, to live, to become.
- Every sentence **must** have a verb.
- Only verbs have tenses. Verbs have different forms of verbs to show if something is happening now or has already happened in the past.

**Examples**

- I swim every day. (*simple present tense*)
- I swam yesterday. (*simple past tense)*
- I am swimming now. (*present progressive)*
- I was swimming yesterday. (*past progressive)*
- She is totally crazy. (*state verb*)
- I am a student. (*state verb*)
- I have a digital watch. (*state verb*)
- I like chocolate ice-cream. (*state verb*)

**Definition**

- Modal verbs are auxiliary or 'helping' verbs that indicate the mood or the attitude of the speaker. They are used to indicate the possibility, ability, permission, obligation or willingness, request, offer . They change the meanings of other verbs (add more information).

- *Examples include can, could, may, might, will, would, shall, should, must, ought to.*

**Examples**

- You must *take off* your shoes before you enter the temple. *(obligation)*

- I will *pay* you tomorrow. *(willingness)*

- Sally can *write* very well. *(ability)*

- Can I help you? *(offer)*

- Shall we *order* a pizza? (offer/suggestion)

- Could you *lend* me a hand please? *(request)*

- I might *clean* the room today. *(possibility)*

- You should *go* to bed on time every day. *(advice)*

- You may *leave* early today. *(permission)*

- It may *snow* tomorrow. *(possibility)*

- Will you like to *paint* with us? *(offer)*

**Definition**

- Imperative verbs create a sentence that gives an order or a command. They are also called bossy verbs as they tell people what to do.

**Examples**

| Sentences | Imperative Instructions |
| --- | --- |
| Please fix the paper with glue. | Fix the paper with glue. |
| It is recommended run for 30 minutes a day. | Run for 30 minutes a day. |
| You will need 2.5 cups of sugar. | Take 2.5 cups of sugar. |
| You must boil it for 10 minutes. | Boil it for 10 minutes. |
| Please shuffle the pack of cards. | Shuffle the pack of cards. |
| You must add a pinch of salt. | Add a pinch of salt. |
| You must line up in the playground. | Line up in the playground. |
| You must fold the paper in half. | Fold the paper in half. |

## Definition

- Adverbs are words that give us more information about

  - the verb (how, when, where) or

  - an adjective or

  - another adverb or

  - a whole clause in the sentence.

- Adverbs generally end in *'ly'* or *'ally'*.

- They can describe the manner (slowly, quietly, angrily etc.), time (later, tonight, early, this year etc.), place (inside, abroad, below etc.) or frequency (always, never, sometimes, usually etc.) of the actions.

## Examples

- Marie *painted* the mural beautifully. *(describes the verb painted)*

- Kevin *solved* the maths problem quickly and accurately. *(describes the verb solved)*

- Anna was quite *sad* to see her test result. *(describes the adjective sad)*

- His mother objected very *strongly* of his plan. *(describes the adverb strongly)*

- The movie was utterly *boring*. *(describes the adjective boring)*

- The exams *start* tomorrow. *(describes when the exams will start)*

- He *rushed* downstairs to open the door. *(describes where he rushed)*

- She often *cooks* on the weekends. *(describes frequency of the action cook)*

**Definition**

- Words that are used to show relationship of a noun or a pronoun to another word. They describe the position or movement of something or the time when something happens or the manner in which it happens. Some prepositions are made of more than one word.

**Examples**

- There is a bird on top of the tree.
- She ran along the river from home to school in thirty minutes with her dog.
- The meeting starts in the conference room at 10am.
- They went to work by train.

**Definition**

- Words that link words, phrases or clauses together in a sentence. They are also called connectives.

- *Example include, and, but, or, nor, for, yet, so, because, if, when, until etc.*

---

**Examples**

- **Coordinating conjunction** joins items of equal importance in a sentence.

  - She likes Maths and Physics.

  - Would you like apples or bananas?

  - Her method was harsh but honest.

  - He is neither good at singing nor dancing.

- **Subordinating conjunction** joins a subordinate clause to the main clause of the sentence.

  - Her mother stayed up until the baby fell asleep.

  - The test was very easy but very time consuming.

  - Although they had their lunch, they were still feeling hungry.

**Definition**

- An interjection is a word or a phrase that is used to express a strong feeling or emotion.
- It is followed by an exclamation mark.

---

**Examples**

- Interjections that show **emotion** include, Wow!, Ouch!, Hoorah! Yippee!, Uh Oh!, Alas!
  - *Hoorah! I won the competition.*
- Interjections that are used as a **greeting** include Hi!, Hey!, Hello!
  - *Hi! How have you been?*
- Interjections that show **agreement/ disagreement** include OK!, yes!, No!, Yeah!, Nah!, Nope!, Sure!
  - *Sure! I will help you with the painting.*
- Interjections that show **sound** include Eek!, Aww!, Argh!, Ugh!, Grr!, Phew!, Yikes!, Shh! Aah! Eww!
  - *Eww! That movie was disgusting.*

**Definition**

- A **Determiner** is a word that introduces a noun and always comes before the noun or the adjective describing the noun. They are required before a singular noun but optional for plural nouns.

- **Articles** are the most common determiners. The three articles are *a*, *an* and *the*. Articles determine which noun the speaker is referring to. 'A' is used before words starting with a consonant or vowels sounding like a consonant. 'An' is used for words starting with a vowel and words beginning with a mute H. 'The' is used before singular and plural nouns (countable or uncountable) when we are talking about something specific or when the noun is mentioned the second time.

**Examples**

- An hour is what I need to finish my homework.

- She won an award for her last song.

- A bird in hand is worth two in the bush.

- I went to the cinema yesterday.

- I stayed at the Ritz during my last travel.

- I am the youngest in my family.

- Hanna is a very studious girl.

- She gave me a useful tip.

**Definition**

- **Main Clause:** A clause that can make sense on its own, it has a subject and a predicate.

- **Subordinate Clause:** A clause that depends on the main clause to make sense. It does not form a complete sentence on its own.

**Examples**

- Kim read all her books until her dad arrived.

- Although he is a fine actor, he has never won any awards.

**Identify different parts of speech for the below sentences:**

1. The weather was remarkably pleasant so they merrily jogged along river Thames in the city.

2. While the boys hungrily ate their warm dinner, we watched an episode of our favourite show on the television.

3. Carl went to the library and diligently finished his homework although he was extremely tired after a tedious and a very long day at school.

4. Rebecca is a master storyteller and packs her stories with unforgettable expressions and voice modulations leaving the listeners spellbound.

5. Anna wants to be a successful pilot so she can frequently fly to different parts of the world.

1. Noun: weather, river, Thames, city; Pronoun: they; Adjective: pleasant; Verb: was, jogged; Adverb: merrily, remarkably; Preposition: along, in; Conjunction: so

2. Noun: boys, television, episode, show, dinner; Pronoun: their, we, our; Adjective: pleasant, favourite, warm; Verb: ate, watched; Adverb: hungrily; Preposition: along, in, on, of; Conjunction: while

3. Noun: Carl, library, homework, day, school; Pronoun: his, he; Adjective: long, tedious, tired; Verb: went, finished, was; Adverb: diligently, extremely, very; Preposition: to, at, after; Conjunction: and, although

4. Noun: Rebecca, storyteller, stories, voice, modulations, expressions, listeners; Pronoun: her; Adjective: master, unforgettable, spellbound; Verb: is, packs, leaving; Preposition: with; Conjunction: and

5. Noun: Anna, pilot, parts, world; Pronoun: she; Adjective: successful, different; Verb: wants, be, can, travel; Adverb: frequently; Preposition: to, of; Conjunction: so

Common articles: a, an, the

**Nice (Adjective)**

- gracious
- amiable
- pleasurable
- genial
- likeable
- approachable
- amusing

- charming
- pleasing
- considerate
- cordial
- courteous
- congenial
- good natured

## Happy (Adjective)

- cheerful

- elated

- contended

- thrilled

- overjoyed

- delighted

- on cloud 9

- ecstatic

- amused

- walking on air

- enthralled

- rapturous

- optimistic

- lively

**Sad (Adjective)**

- miserable

- gloomy

- frustrated

- tearful

- downcast

- despairing

- sorrowful

- dispirited

- sombre

- despondent

- devastated

- anguished

- bereaved

- grief-stricken

**Pretty (Adjective)**

- gorgeous

- sensational

- graceful

- out of this world

- stunning

- mesmerising

- exquisite

- dazzling

- appealing

- enchanting

- attractive

- alluring

- charming

- prepossessing

## Bad (Adjective)

- deficient

- atrocious

- awful

- rotten

- dreadful

- wretched

- wicked

- inferior

- unacceptable

- mean

- nasty

- disagreeable

- unpleasant

- dissatisfactory

**Angry (Adjective)**

- irate

- enraged

- resentful

- infuriated

- wound up

- worked up

- aggravated

- spiteful

- violent

- livid

- inflamed

- disagreeable

- indignant

- distressed

**Big (Adjective)**

- considerable
- extensive
- massive
- gigantic
- vast
- substantial
- enormous

- colossal
- immense
- monumental
- epic
- gargantuan
- mammoth
- stupendous

## Small (Adjective)

- tiny

- skimpy

- minute

- minuscule

- infinitesimal

- microscopic

- slender

- petite

- compact

- midget

- puny

- cosy

- unimportant

- insignificant

**Awesome (Adjective)**

- fascinating

- stunning

- incredible

- marvellous

- wonderful

- astonishing

- breath-taking

- stupendous

- awe-inspiring

- extraordinary

- unbelievable

- remarkable

- phenomenal

- spectacular

**Funny (Adjective)**

- amusing

- gleeful

- comical

- hilarious

- entertaining

- whimsical

- humorous

- ludicrous

- jocular

- mirthful

- laughable

- entertaining

- witty

- light-hearted

**Run (Verb)**

- dart
- race
- dash
- rush
- jog
- scurry
- sprint

- scamper
- scuttle
- scramble
- charge
- bustle
- hurry
- hasten

# Vocabulary Builder

216

## A lot (Adjective)

- copious

- plentiful

- myriad

- generous

- bountiful

- opulent

- prolific

- countless

- several

- numerous

- cornucopia

- plethora

- abundant

- ample

**Like (Verb)**

- enjoy
- cherish
- relish
- revere
- admire
- appreciate
- adore

- savour
- treasure
- fond of
- revel in
- hold dear
- worship
- honour

**Said (Verb)**

- announced

- revealed

- expressed

- described

- uttered

- divulged

- disclosed

- babbled

- jabbered

- gossiped

- recited

- pronounced

- vocalized

- commented

## Change (Verb)

- transform
- switch
- modify
- transition
- revise
- adjust
- alter

- convert
- metamorphose
- transfigure
- restyle
- reorganize
- remould
- revamp

## Easy (Adjective)

- uncomplicated
- effortless
- straightforward
- painless
- undemanding
- elementary
- unchallenging

## Easy going (Adjective)

- nonchalant
- relaxed
- mellow
- unruffled
- carefree
- poised
- placid

## Scared (Adjective)

- uneasy

- horrified

- jumpy

- alarmed

- terrorised

- nervous

- phobic

- perturbed

- shaky

- startled

- paralyzed

- petrified

- rattled

- hysterical

## Anxious (Adjective)

- apprehensive
- fretful
- perturbed
- insecure
- stressed
- overwrought
- tense

- timid
- troubled
- fidgety
- edgy
- hesitant
- flurried
- frantic

**Stating your opinion**

- in my opinion
- from my perspective
- I understand
- in my view
- I realize
- I feel
- it seems to me that
- I imagine
- I suppose

**Giving Examples**

- for example
- that is
- namely
- such as
- to illustrate
- for instance
- as
- as revealed by
- in the case of

**Comparing**

- similar to
- neither… nor
- in the same way
- in common
- just as
- at the same time
- either…. or
- as is
- also

## Expressing Partial Agreement

- more or less
- to some extent
- up to a point
- almost
- in a way
- so to speak

## Concluding

- to sum up
- in conclusion
- all things considered
- taking everything into consideration
- weighing up both sides of the argument
- the advantages of…. outweigh the disadvantages

## Expressing certainty

- certainly
- undoubtedly
- doubtless
- no doubt
- definitely
- of course

# Comma Rules

**Commas do not just signify pauses in a sentence but also help us write clearly. Please find below few rules to use commas effectively. Use a comma(s):**

☑ Before the conjunction (and, but, for, or, nor, so, yet) in a compound sentence to separate independent clauses.
*Reema likes to paint, and she likes to dance.*

☑ After introductory clauses, phrases, or words that come before the main clause.
*While we were eating, she finished her painting.*

☑ To separate words that are not part of the sentence.
*Unfortunately, he lost his phone.*

☑ In the middle of a sentence to separate clauses, phrases and words that are not essential to the meaning of the sentence. If these words are dropped, the sentences will make sense retain its basic meaning.
*We are, as you can sense, very excited about the holiday.*

☑ When beginning sentences with introductory words such as well, now, yes.
*Yes, I do need that coffee.*

☑ In a list of three or more items (words, phrases or clauses) joined by 'and', 'or' or 'nor.
*I like to play football, cricket and tennis.*

☑ Before and after quotation marks to separate direct quotation from the rest of the sentence.
*"I like to play football", I said.*

**Identify and place the commas effectively for the below sentences.**

1. They offered him an ice-cream and he accepted it immediately.
2. We need a canvas paintbrushes and paint to make a painting.
3. While we swam he finished his homework.
4. Sadly he did not win the lottery.
5. If you practice every day you will be a swimmer in no time.
6. You will be a swimmer in no time if you practice every day.
7. They were as you can see cheating to get in.
8. I was so angry when I heard the news!
9. Well I am very hopeful about the new government.
10. I like to play football cricket and tennis.
11. I said "I want to read the book".
12. That boy is a genius who won the science competition.
13. My sister whom you met at my house just had a baby.
14. We can cook dinner or we can just order in a takeaway.

1.  They offered him an ice-cream, and he accepted it immediately.

2.  We need a canvas, paintbrushes and paint to make a painting.

3.  While we swam, he finished his homework.

4.  Sadly, he did not win the lottery.

5.  If you practice every day, you will be a swimmer in no time.

6.  You will be a swimmer in no time if you practice every day. *(no comma required as dependent or subordinate clause comes after the main clause).*

7.  They were, as you can see, cheating to win.

8.  I was so angry when I heard the news! *(no comma required as dependent or subordinate clause comes after the main clause).*

9.  Well, I am very hopeful about the new government.

10. I like to play football, cricket and tennis.

11.  I said, "I want to read the book".

12. That boy is a genius who won the science competition. *(no comma required as the subordinate clause is an essential relative clause).*

13. My sister, whom you met at my house, just had a baby.

14. We can cook today, or order in a takeaway.

# How to Proofread?

**Steps**

Your piece of writing is incomplete without proofreading. Proofreading means checking for errors in **s**pelling, **p**unctuation and **g**rammar. It can be difficult to spot errors in your own writing. Below steps will help you to proofread your work.

- Read your work out loud pointing at each word while reading.
- Read it backwards as it helps you to focus on each word and spot spelling errors.
- Create your own checklist – include your common mistakes or bad habits.

**Checklist Example**

☑ Words are spelt correctly.

☑ Sentences are complete, clear and easy to understand.

☑ Sentences end in a full stop/ question mark/ exclamation mark.

☑ Commas are used appropriately.

☑ Capitals are used appropriately.

☑ The sentences and paragraphs connect well and are clearly structured.

☑ Direct quotations and paraphrases are used effectively.

☑ If writing in the first person, the entire text is written in the first person. Similarly, if you are writing in the second and third person.

☑ Consistent use of verb tense throughout the writing.

☑ Effective use and choice of words – clear, vivid and precise words; avoiding clichés and overused words/expressions.